the fondue bible

the
fondue
bible

the **200** best recipes

ILANA SIMON

For complete cataloguing information, see page 257.

Disclaimer
The recipes in this book have been carefully tested by our kitchen and our tasters. To the best
of our knowledge, they are safe and nutritious for ordinary use and users. For those people with food
or other allergies, or who have special food requirements or health issues, please read the suggested
contents of each recipe carefully and determine whether or not they may create a problem for you.
All recipes are used at the risk of the consumer.

We cannot be responsible for any hazards, loss or damage that may occur as a result of any
recipe use.

For those with special needs, allergies, requirements or health problems, in the event of any
doubt, please contact your medical advisor prior to the use of any recipe.

Design & Production: Daniella Zanchetta/PageWave Graphics Inc.
Editor: Sue Sumeraj
Proofreader: Sheila Wawanash
Indexer: Gillian Watts
Photography: Mark Shapiro and Colin Erricson
Food Styling: Kate Bush
Prop Styling: Charlene Erricson

Cover image: Emmentaler-Gruyère Fondue with Roasted Garlic (see recipe, page 31)

We acknowledge the financial support of the Government of Canada through the Book Publishing
Industry Development Program (BPIDP) for our publishing activities.

Published by Robert Rose Inc.
120 Eglinton Avenue East, Suite 800
Toronto, Ontario, Canada M4P 1E2
Tel: (416) 322-6552   Fax: (416) 322-6936

Printed in Canada
1 2 3 4 5 6 7 8 9 TCP 15 14 13 12 11 10 09 08 07

To my husband, Ari Marantz.

Contents

Acknowledgments

THE FONDUE BIBLE WOULD NOT have come about without the insight and wisdom of publisher Bob Dees. Thank you for providing invaluable guidance and encouragement in making *The Fondue Bible* a reality.

Kudos to the design and production team at PageWave Graphics Inc. — Andrew Smith, Joseph Gisini, Kevin Cockburn and Daniella Zanchetta — for making *The Fondue Bible* so incredibly engaging and appealing.

Cheers to the professionals behind the scenes: Mark T. Shapiro and Colin Ericson for their fabulous fondue photography; Kate Bush for her tantalizing food styling; Charlene Ericson for her charming prop styling; Sheila Wawanash for proofreading; and Gillian Watts for the index. And a big thank you to editor Sue "Superfantastic" Sumeraj.

I am grateful to recipe tester Cheryl Warkentin for once again cheerfully and efficiently testing many of my recipes. I also want to thank my extended family and friends who supported me on this latest fondue frenzy. Creating recipes for *The Fondue Bible* resulted in many fun fondue parties and memorable meals. Last, but definitely not least, a special thanks to my husband, Ari Marantz, and sons, Jesse and Evan. My home team is always there for me — and willing to sample new recipes with their sense of adventure and discriminating taste buds. You demonstrated that, even with teenagers, fondue can be a fun family affair!

Introduction

THERE'S SOMETHING UNIQUE about sharing a fondue with family and friends around your table. Everyone is relaxed — including the host — and the pace of the intimate meal is as leisurely as you want.

For anyone old enough to remember the 1970s, the fondue also carries with it a certain nostalgia. Remember those college and après ski fondue parties? The obligatory fondue pot given as a bridal shower or wedding gift? Well, fondues are back, and once again, it's hip to dip!

In recent years, sales of fondue pots — ranging from traditional flame-burning fondues to the sleek, new, easy-to-use electric versions — have skyrocketed. You'll find them everywhere, on cookware websites and on the shelves of kitchen stores. Restaurants devoted to fondue have cropped up around North America, and new generations are discovering the allure of the fondue tradition.

Fonduing is a fun and easy way to entertain and is more sociable than your typical dinner party. But you needn't wait for a special occasion to get retro and partake in no-fuss fondue. In today's fast-paced world, a romantic, lingering fondue for two offers an opportunity to enjoy one another's company while savoring melted comfort food.

Fondue is also an ideal way to spend quality time together as a family, and kids of all ages love to participate in cooking their own food — especially when it involves chocolate! But don't discount other unhurried fondues with the junior set. Try dishes such as Pizza Fondue (page 57), Child-Friendly Mexican Fondue (page 49), Chicken Nuggets oil fondue (page 103), "Fried" Mars Bar Fondue (page 121) and Shrimp in Mexican Broth (page 188), to name a few.

Today's fondue goes well beyond the standard duo of cheese and chocolate — though I have included an array of traditional fondue dishes such as Classic Swiss Cheese Fondue (page 28) and Classic Beef Bourguignonne (page 78). But international cooking styles present a plethora of fondue possibilities, such as Mongolian Hot Pot (page 160), Japanese Sukiyaki (page 142) and tempura (page 120), spicy Indian curries and Mexican bubbling cheese fondues, as well as simmering Middle Eastern, Thai and Italian broths. And unlike the fondues of yesterday — never exactly low in fat — many of the new varieties have a healthier twist, with fresh foods swished in flavorful broths instead of oil. One of my all-time favorite fondues in *The Fondue Bible* is the

Paella Fondue (page 144), a sensational broth fondue that takes its inspiration from saffron-infused paella and is the ideal centerpiece at a fondue party.

Still, cheese and oil fondues continue to play an important role in creating a contemporary fondue feast. So, in addition to dipping French bread into creamy Swiss cheese fondue or spearing beef tenderloin into sizzling hot oil, with the recipes in this book you can indulge in Truffle Fondue (page 55) or Smoked Salmon and Cream Cheese Fondue (page 64), or take a stab at Coconut Shrimp (page 112) or Moroccan Meatball (page 91) oil fondues.

And don't forget that, despite our culture's calorie-counting obsession, decadent desserts still reign supreme — and in moderation, why not? Chocolate lovers will be thrilled by the extensive compilation of dessert fondues in this book, including various types of chocolate paired with complementary flavors such as maple, cherry, coffee, peanut butter and mint. You'll even find a delicious Diabetic Chocolate Fondue (page 211) that holds its own. Also included is a dizzying array of other sweet sensations, ranging from caramel to rum and butter to key lime.

Ultimately, fonduing is all about fun and relaxation. For the host, a fondue party requires only a little shopping, chopping, marinating and grating. After that, it's the guests who do the work: cooking, dipping, dunking and devouring.

Fire, food and friendship appeal to our primitive urges — think cavemen and cavewomen huddling around a campfire, spearing meat and cooking over fire. A fondue party offers a chance to recreate (well, kind of) this fabled scenario. It's a cozy meal focused on a pot over fire in which guests cook their skewered meat while enjoying good conversation, good food and good times.

Enjoy!

Ilana Simon

Fondue Essentials

Fondues past and present

STEMMING FROM THE FRENCH WORD *fondre*, meaning "to melt," fondue has come a long way since the first cheese version was invented centuries ago by the Swiss. Like many food discoveries, it was the result of practical necessity. Isolated alpine villagers, as well as traveling sheep and goat herders, relied mainly on provisions of cheese, wine and bread to sustain themselves during the long winters. Often the cheese made in summer had dried out by winter. To use up the hardened cheese and stale bread, the Swiss would melt cheese with wine over fire and dunk in pieces of bread for a warm, satisfying meal.

Since fonduing caught on in North America, the term "fondue" has been applied to all foods (melted or otherwise) cooked in a single pot at the table and then dipped into sauces. But there are some important differences between the different types of fondue.

The Swiss region of Neuchâtel is credited with the birth of cheese fondues based on Gruyère and Emmentaler — and this combination still provides the foundation for the Classic Swiss Cheese Fondue recipe in this book (see page 28). But just as different Swiss villages devised their own cheese fondue versions based on local products, my collection of cheese fondues reflects cheese and flavors from around the world. And luckily, globalization has meant the ready availability of imported cheese and other ingredients — most of which can be found at your local supermarket.

The origin of oil fondue, called fondue bourguignonne (Burgundian fondue), is disputed. One version claims it originated in the vineyards of the Burgundy region of France. Workers had little time to eat while in the fields harvesting grapes and the winery owners grappled with how to feed everyone a hot meal at once. To meet this challenge, owners placed heated pots of grapeseed oil in the fields to allow the grape pickers an opportunity to eat whenever they were hungry. The workers brought pouches of meat from home and could simply spear the meat and cook it quickly in the hot oil. This swift meal meant workers could return to the fields quickly (after a hearty, hot meal) and harvest the grapes at their peak of ripeness.

A less romantic tale pinpoints the development of fondue Bourguignonne to sometime after World War II by French-speaking Swiss chefs who sought another option to the traditional cheese fondue.

They began cooking meat in hot oil and, since the French-speaking Swiss are descendants of Burgundians, this method of fondue was named "fondue bourguignonne."

Broth fondues, on the other hand, are a direct adaptation of the Mongolian fire pot. This centuries-old cooking method uses a round pot with a chimney in the center, under which coal is placed to heat the contents of the pot. Lamb and vegetables were traditionally cooked in the steaming broth. The collection of broth fondue recipes in this book includes those that are linked closely to their Asian origins, as well as a range of other international cooking styles, ranging from Latin to Moroccan.

Chocolate fondue is said to have originated at a press conference in New York in 1966 where a Swiss chocolate bar manufacturer demonstrated how its product could be melted and served with pieces of fruit, cake and cookies for dipping. It caught on with New York restaurants and, later, at European ski resorts. Today chocolate fondue appears on many restaurant menus (including non-fondue restaurants) and is one of the best known and most popular of all fondues.

In this book, you'll find many simple recipes for the neophyte, as well as an extensive catalogue of fondue possibilities for those who are experienced in this cooking method and want to broaden their fondue horizons.

Choosing and using fondue equipment

THERE ARE MANY STYLES and varieties of fondue sets on the market today, featuring myriad colors, shapes, sizes and designs for specific uses.

In general, every fondue set includes a pot, a stand on which the pot rests and a heat source located beneath the pot for keeping the fondue hot or warm. With traditional fondue sets, the heat is usually supplied by an alcohol burner (for cheese, broth and oil fondues) or votive candle (for chocolate and other dessert fondues).

Denatured alcohol or fondue fuel can be used interchangeably in alcohol burners. Never add fondue fuel to a lit burner and always carefully fill and light the burner only when it is in place on the fondue stand. Light the burner with a match, never a lighter. Keep the cover of the alcohol burner on hand at all times to extinguish the flame if need be.

Electric fondue sets are another practical alternative — particularly for oil and broth fondues. These units often feature nonstick surfaces (making them effortless to clean) and offer uncomplicated temperature controls.

When using an electric fondue, be sure to have a sufficiently long extension cord to avoid anyone tripping over it and knocking the fondue over. If children are present, they should be adequately supervised.

No matter what type of fondue set you use, the number of people using it should not exceed six. Should your guest list exceed this number, prepare additional fondue pots. This helps to avoid too many people reaching for one pot (and the spills that may result). Always place the fondue pot on a heat-resistant surface (such as a baking stone or heatproof trivet) in the center of the table. This will also minimize the risk of accidentally spilling lit fuel and starting a fire.

Finally, be sure to read the fondue pot's instruction manual before using, and exercise caution whenever transferring hot oil or broth from the stove to the fondue pot.

What to use for cheese fondues

EARTHENWARE, CERAMIC OR ENAMELED cast-iron pots are ideal for cheese fondues because the material diffuses the heat and helps to prevent scorching of the delicate cheese fondue. Never fondue cheese in a metal fondue pot! Metal conducts heat and is likely to result in burnt cheese.

Most ceramic or earthenware fondue pots should not be heated on a stove element unless otherwise stated by the manufacturer. Enameled cast-iron fondue pots, on the other hand, are suitable for use on your stove's heating element. Cheese fondue can then easily be prepared in the fondue pot and simply transferred to the stand once melted. Otherwise, cheese fondue should be prepared in a saucepan and carefully transferred to the fondue pot. Keep in mind, too, that cheese fondues can scorch easily and should be kept warm over a low flame to avoid burning.

The earthenware or ceramic fondue pot resembles the original Swiss *caquelon* used for cheese fondue, which was shaped like a shallow casserole with a handle, and provided ample surface area for swirling of cheese — an important function to keep the cheese creamy.

Slow cookers can also be used for cheese fondue, both for cooking the fondue itself and for keeping it warm at the table.

What to use for oil fondues

OIL FONDUE POTS ARE MADE of metal, usually stainless steel or copper, which transfers the heat evenly and keeps the oil hot while fonduing. Never use a ceramic or earthenware cheese fondue pot for oil! The hot oil will break the pot and can be very dangerous. Enameled cast-iron, however, can be used for oil fondues.

All aspects of oil fondues require caution when using the traditional short-handled metal fondue bourguignonne pot. First, you must heat the oil in a saucepan on the stove, observing constantly until it becomes still, just under boiling, at 375°F (190°C). You can check the temperature with a deep-frying thermometer. Transfer the oil carefully to the fondue pot set on a baking stone or heatproof trivet, being sure that you do not fill it more than half full. Periodically check the temperature of the oil during the course of the fondue. The flame must be strong enough to maintain the heat at 360°F (185°C) to 375°F (190°C).

A much simpler alternative (and one that I recommend) for oil fondues is the electric fondue pot. Here the oil is heated to the correct temperature in one pot (no need to transfer it from a saucepan, heated on the stove), and it is much easier to maintain the correct temperature.

What type of oil should you use? Peanut oil, with its high smoking point, is ideal. But it is very expensive, and I have found that canola or vegetable oil works equally well. I suggest that you experiment with different oils (or shortening) to determine your personal preference.

Finally, keep in mind that fondue forks get very hot when submerged in oil. Food should be removed from the tines, patted on a paper towel to remove excess oil (if desired), and then eaten with a regular fork.

What to use for broth fondues

FOR BROTH FONDUES, sometimes called fondue chinoise or Asian fire pot, use either metal or electric fondue pots. If you wish to be truly authentic, you can use a real Chinese hot pot (available at Asian specialty stores). Slow cookers can also be adapted for use with broth fondues.

Broth fondues typically involve bringing the broth to a rolling boil on the stovetop and then carefully transferring it to the fondue pot. With traditional fondue sets, the broth is kept at a simmer with an alcohol burner, with the flame set to medium or medium-low. Electric fondues allow you to control the temperature automatically. If using a slow cooker, follow the manufacturer's directions and prepare the broth directly in the slow cooker; the temperature should be set to minimum during the fondue.

What to use for dessert fondues

BECAUSE THEY ARE SO DELICATE, chocolate or dessert fondues require equipment that will prevent its contents from scorching. Typically, these fondue sets consist of a small ceramic pot set over a votive candle (not an alcohol burner), providing just enough heat to keep the sweet sauce warm. Chocolate is particularly vulnerable to scorching, so a cheese fondue set, even with the flame turned to low, will be too hot. For other dessert fondues that are less likely to scorch, a cheese fondue set over a very low flame may be acceptable.

Dessert fondue forks are smaller than cheese and oil fondue forks. Each guest only requires one fondue fork, a regular fork and dessert bowl. (A bowl is essential for runny sauces or where children are involved). The dipper, usually fruit or a plain cake, is merely dunked in the chocolate or other sweet sauce, removed from the fondue fork into the bowl and enjoyed.

A word about fondue utensils

LONG METAL FONDUE FORKS with heat-resistant handles are essential for fonduing (especially those using hot oil). Most fondue fork handles are color-keyed for easy identification of individual diners' forks. Supply each person with one fondue fork for a cheese fondue, and two for oil or broth fondues. (When one comes out, the other goes in.) Try to provide each person with forks of the same color.

Never use a plain metal skewer in place of a fondue fork, since it will conduct heat to the fingers. Wooden bamboo skewers can be used in a pinch, although they become charred quickly, making it difficult to distinguish which skewer belongs to whom.

In addition to fondue fork(s), provide each guest with conventional forks and knives alongside their dinner plates. Use these to eat oil-cooked meat or fish (since fondue forks are often too hot to bring food to the mouth) and for side dishes such as salad and rice.

Also provide each guest with a separate bowl in which to place raw meat taken from a serving platter. This will minimize the chance that bacteria-laden raw meat will come into contact with the dinner plate on which the cooked meat will be eaten.

Many fondue sets come with a range of sauce dishes (these are also sold separately) that greatly complement the fondue table. Otherwise, use any small glass or ceramic bowls to showcase a variety of dipping sauces. Fondue plates, featuring separate compartments for foods and sauce, are also available.

If you are a fan of Asian hot pot–style fondues, a long-handled Chinese wire basket is an important accessory for fishing out pieces of beef and vegetables.

Firing up the fondue menu

FONDUING BASICALLY INVOLVES dipping crusty bread chunks in melted cheese and wine sauce; cooking meat, poultry or seafood in oil or broth until rare or done according to personal preference; and dunking fruit, cookie and cake pieces into chocolate or other sweet sauces for dessert. Dips play a starring role on a fondue dinner table and a minimum of four should be on hand for a fondue party.

Once everyone is seated around the informal table featuring a palette of dips and sauces, and long-handled fondue forks are at the ready, the fun of the fondue ritual really begins.

A typical fondue party begins with cheese fondue, followed by main-course broth and oil fondues, and is then completed with a luscious chocolate fondue of your choosing.

Meat, poultry and seafood go a long way in a fondue meal. One pound (500 g) of beef, pork, chicken, veal or seafood is adequate to feed four adults, assuming that you will be serving other side dishes and an appetizer cheese fondue. For a cheese fondue, plan on 1 large loaf of crusty Italian or French bread for a party of four. It works out to approximately 4 slices (cubed) per person.

Unless otherwise stated, all of the recipes in *The Fondue Bible* will serve four.

Since fondue is not a quick cooking method, be sure to provide enough side dishes to keep your hungry guests satisfied as they wait. A hearty salad, steamed vegetables (also good for dipping in cheese fondues), steamed rice (or rice pilaf), pasta or boiled new potatoes (another good dipper in cheese) will round out the fondue table.

A variety of homemade and/or store-bought sauces and condiments will help to complete the fondue experience. Mix global flavors for an eclectic evening or follow a theme (for example, a "Mexican night").

Four Fondue Fables

1. When a woman drops a piece of bread into the cheese fondue pot, she is supposed to kiss the man closest to her on the left.

2. When a man drops a piece of bread into the pot, he is expected to buy the next bottle of wine, pot of fondue or round of drinks for the table.

3. When the cheese fondue is nearly complete, you will notice a golden brown crust forming on the bottom of the pot. This is considered the best part of the cheese fondue and should be carefully scraped from the pot and presented to an honored guest — or divided up among guests, giving each person a chance to sample the divine crispy cheese.

4. It is considered bad form to immediately rise from the table once the fondue flame has extinguished. Instead, wait a few moments and serve brandy with leftover bits of bread and, later, coffee or a chilled sweet wine.

Choosing beverages to accompany fondues

TRADITIONALLY, CHILLED BEVERAGES were not considered appropriate accompaniments to hot (especially cheese) fondues. Preferred choices were hot black tea, mulled wine or kirsch (cherry schnapps — an ingredient often used in the fondue). Serious fondue ritual often called for the beverage to be served only at the halfway point of the meal.

Today, of course, we tend to be a little more relaxed about things, and it's very common to enjoy wine with fondues — preferably the same wine (or beer) used in the fondue preparation, served at room temperature or just slightly chilled. If you are partaking in the fondue as a "back to the '70s" experience, try serving sangria — the quintessential beverage of that decade.

You may find, as I have, that a number of red wines go remarkably well with cheese fondues. But as with all types of entertaining, use your personal preference as a guide to your choice of beverages.

What to do with leftovers

ALTHOUGH IT DOESN'T HAPPEN very often, you will sometimes have leftovers following a fondue meal. Don't throw them out, since they have plenty of uses. Extra cheese fondue, for example, can be reheated and used to make macaroni and cheese or as a topping on baked potatoes.

Oil from fondues can be reused once or twice, but may need to be strained. Food particles tend to fall into the oil during fonduing and can present a hazard during reheating.

Broths make ideal lunches. Add soaked rice stick noodles, any leftover meat or seafood or vegetables, simmer for a few minutes in the fondue pot, and voila — a hearty, tasty soup.

Chocolate or other dessert fondues can be reheated in the microwave and poured over ice cream or bread pudding, or simply reheated and enjoyed once again with fruit or other dippers. As well, apples or other fruit can be dipped into remaining chocolate or caramel fondue, refrigerated on a baking sheet and enjoyed once cooled.

Adapting your favorite recipes for the fondue

A FAVORITE SOUP CAN BE transformed into a fondue broth by defining the distinguishing flavors, adding the specific herbs, spices and other flavor enhancers to chicken or beef broth, and simmering the ingredients for 15 minutes to infuse the flavors.

Oil fondues work best with battered foods. If you have a favorite batter recipe, try using it to coat cubes of beef, pork, lamb, veal, chicken or seafood, then cooking it in an oil fondue. Remember to bring the battered foods to room temperature before fonduing.

Cheese fondue is a little trickier to adapt from traditional recipes. But once you become comfortable with the method of combining the main ingredients (wine, cheese, cornstarch and lemon juice), you can try adding other flavor enhancers, experimenting with different cheeses, and using beer or cider in place of wine.

Dessert fondues provide perhaps the greatest opportunity for being creative. Try taking a favorite dessert sauce and turning it into a dessert fondue. Depending on the sauce, you may need to thicken it with cornstarch so that it will adhere to fruit and other dippers, or add cream to thin it out, or adjust the cooking time so that it reaches the right consistency for dipping.

Fon-Do's (and Don'ts)

1. Read the manufacturer's instruction manual prior to using your fondue pot for the first time.

2. Before using a new ceramic or enameled cast-iron fondue pot, fill it with a mixture of half water and half milk; boil for 15 minutes. Now your fondue pot is ready.

3. Position the fondue stand on a heatproof mat, trivet, ceramic tile or baking stone on the table.

4. Situate the burner in its place and fill near to the top (do not overfill) with denatured alcohol, fondue fuel or fondue paste. Use alcohol, fuel or paste according to manufacturer's recommendations.

5. Light the burner with a match (not a lighter), and never refill the burner while it is lit. Alcohol burners typically hold 3 oz (75 mL) denatured alcohol fuel, which will last for about 1½ hours. Extinguish the burner with burner cover when necessary.

6. Fondue paste burners appear similar to alcohol burners but are equipped for paste or gel containers, or bulk gel that is poured into the burner. This fuel is less likely to spill. Never add paste while the burner is lit. Use paste or gel only in burners designed for fuel paste.

7. Flare-ups are unlikely but can occur with tabletop fondue pots. A sturdy fondue pot and sturdy table reduce the chances of accidental tipping of the burners.

8. Always keep the burner cover at hand should you need to smother the flame quickly. Having a fire extinguisher close by is an added safety precaution.

9. Select the appropriate pot for your fondue — a large ceramic or enameled cast-iron pot for cheese, a stainless steel or copper pot for oil fondues, and small ceramic pots for desserts. The new generation of fondue pots are sturdier and more versatile than the wobbly ones of the past.

10. Check the manufacturer's instructions on whether the fondue pot can be heated on a kitchen range. It's so much easier to cook the fondue in its own pot on the stove, and then simply transfer it to the fondue stand for serving.

11. If using a non-electric fondue, oil must be heated on the stovetop before transferring it to the fondue stand. It should be heated to 375°F (190°C), just below the boiling point.

12. Wear oven mitts and exercise caution when moving or transferring hot pots from the stovetop to fondue stands.

13. Never try to serve more than six people from one fondue pot. Always equip each person with an adequate number of color-coded fondue forks and plenty of napkins, as well as regular dinner plates and utensils.

14. Wash ceramic and earthenware pots by hand in hot, soapy water. Do not use steel wool, but rather a plastic brush or scrubber if necessary. Allow cheese fondue pots to soak before washing. Check manufacturer's instructions to see if the pot is dishwasher-safe.

15. A cheese fondue requires an acidic cooking liquid like a dry white wine to aid in breaking down the cheese proteins for melting. Freshly squeezed lemon juice is often added to achieve the necessary acidity.

16. Not every cheese melts well, or marries well. If you're experimenting, keep in mind that a strong cheese may overpower a milder one.

17. Fondue inspires creativity in the areas of dippers (it doesn't have to be baguette every time for cheese) and in dipping sauces. Let your creative juices flow and take fondue a step further. Dip marinated artichokes in a smooth cheese, for example, or cooked cubes of sausage in a Mexican fondue.

18. Dessert fondues encompass a huge variety of melted chocolate blends, as well as other sweet treats in which to dip mainly fruit, pieces of plain cake or ladyfingers. When dipping fruit in chocolate, make sure there is no excess water on the fruit or the chocolate may seize.

Cheese fondues

Cheese fondues

Ingredients

WHILE THERE ARE MANY different types of cheese fondues (as you'll discover in this chapter), almost all are based on the combination of one or more cheeses (mostly strong-tasting varieties) balanced against liquid ingredients — such as dry white wine, beer, cider, lemon or lime juice, or a fruit spirit such as kirsch — which provide both acidity and flavor.

Many of the recipes in this chapter use the famous Swiss cheeses (such as Gruyère and Emmentaler), but I have also found success with other cheeses such as Asiago, Brie, Cheddar, cream cheese, fontina, goat cheese, Monterey Jack, Parmesan, and others.

The liquids in the recipes often contain alcohol, which lowers the boiling point in fondues so that cheese proteins won't curdle. (Even so, the cheese fondue should never boil.) If you decide to double a cheese fondue recipe for a larger crowd, keep in mind there is less surface area to evaporate liquids, so do not quite double the liquids of the original recipe.

Preparation

LIQUIDS CALLED FOR in cheese fondues (dry white wine or beer, for example) should be used at room temperature. The liquid should be brought to just below boiling over medium heat; then, after reducing the heat slightly, the cheese is added.

Typically, the cheese will have been grated or cubed and tossed with cornstarch or flour before it is added by handfuls to the simmering liquid. After each addition, the cheese should be stirred in a figure-eight pattern with a wooden spoon until it is melted.

Cheese fondue should never boil or it will become stringy. If it does become stringy, turn the heat to low and continue stirring until the cheese is creamy.

If the cheese separates during preparation (or during the fondue meal), heat it over medium heat, whisking constantly, until it combines and becomes smooth.

If the cheese is too thick, stir in warm wine, beer or cider to thin out the sauce. If your cheese fondue is too thin, add more of the grated cheese you are using (start with 1/4 cup/50 mL) or dissolve 1 to 2 teaspoons (5 to

10 mL) cornstarch in 1 tbsp (15 mL) wine or lemon juice and slowly whisk into fondue.

If the cheese is lumpy, add 1 tsp (5 mL) lemon or lime juice and slowly whisk in until smooth.

In the fondue pot

ALWAYS MAKE CHEESE FONDUE in an earthenware or enameled cast-iron pot to avoid burning.

When you carefully transfer your cheese fondue to the fondue pot, ensure the flame is on low and that the cheese is only gently bubbling (or it will burn).

To keep cheese creamy during the fondue meal, stir the fondue frequently in a figure-eight pattern with your fondue fork while dunking in a cube of bread (and suggest guests do the same). If the fondue is swirled each time a diner dips in bread, it will stay creamy.

Also gently scrape the bottom of the fondue pot occasionally to prevent the cheese from burning. When the fondue is finished, allow the remaining cheese to cool and then scrape off the golden-brown crispy cheese for a special treat to be given to a guest of honor or shared among guests.

Serving the fondue

BREAD SERVED WITH CHEESE fondue should not be too fresh, but not stale either. Slice the bread just before serving, allowing about 1 loaf of bread for every four people.

Cheese fondues work admirably with crusty Italian or French bread, but there are many other prospective partners, such as seven-grain, sourdough, egg, pumpernickel or rye breads, pita, bread sticks, focaccia, bagel, or English muffins. Cut bread for fonduing into 1-inch (2.5 cm) cubes or triangles, with a little crust on each piece. Spear each cube at the crust for best fonduing results.

Cheese fondues are also delicious with steamed vegetables — especially asparagus, broccoli, cauliflower and mushrooms — as well as fresh cherry tomatoes, zucchini sticks, red pepper slices and celery sticks.

Other dippers for cheese fondues include tortilla chips, salami chunks, crackers, and pretzels.

Classic Swiss Cheese Fondue

Here's the original Swiss cheese fondue that has inspired so many other wonderful variations. Be sure to purchase Swiss Emmentaler cheese and Gruyère cheese. Nothing else is quite as good.

Tips
Freshly grated nutmeg makes a big difference in flavor. Look for whole nutmeg in specialty food stores and grate it finely.

Once in the fondue pot, stir cheese occasionally in a figure-eight motion to prevent scorching.

Make ahead
Grate Emmentaler and Gruyère and combine in a bowl; refrigerate until needed.

Serve with...
Traditional accompaniments: crusty cubes of French or Italian bread.

8 oz	Emmentaler cheese, grated	250 g
8 oz	Gruyère cheese, grated	250 g
1	clove garlic, halved	1
1 cup	dry white wine	250 mL
1 tbsp	freshly squeezed lemon juice	15 mL
3 tbsp	kirsch (dry cherry schnapps)	45 mL
1 tbsp	cornstarch	15 mL
Pinch	freshly ground white pepper	Pinch
Pinch	ground nutmeg	Pinch

1. In a bowl, combine Emmentaler and Gruyère; mix well. Set aside.

2. Rub the inside of a large saucepan with cut sides of garlic. Discard garlic. Add wine and lemon juice; bring to a simmer over medium heat. Reduce heat to medium-low.

3. Add cheese mixture in small amounts to saucepan, whisking constantly after each addition in a figure-eight motion until cheese is melted.

4. In a small bowl, whisk together kirsch and cornstarch until smooth; stir into melted cheese. Season with white pepper and nutmeg, stirring until smooth. Transfer to fondue pot and serve immediately.

Gruyère Fondue with Toasted Almonds

6 oz	Emmentaler cheese, grated	175 g
6 oz	Gruyère cheese, grated	175 g
2 tsp	all-purpose flour	10 mL
¾ cup	dry white wine	175 mL
1 tbsp	freshly squeezed lemon juice	15 mL
¼ cup	slivered almonds, toasted (see tip, at right) and chopped	50 mL

1. In a bowl, combine Emmentaler, Gruyère and flour; mix well to coat cheese with flour. Set aside.

2. In a large saucepan, combine white wine and lemon juice; bring to a simmer over medium heat. Reduce heat to medium-low.

3. Add cheese mixture by handfuls to saucepan, stirring constantly after each addition with a wooden spoon in a figure-eight motion until cheese is melted. Transfer to fondue pot and stir in toasted almonds. Serve immediately.

Serves 4

Tip

To toast almonds: Place almonds on baking sheet and toast in a preheated 350°F (180°C) oven for about 5 minutes, turning once, until golden (not dark) brown. Alternatively, toast almonds in nonstick skillet over medium heat, turning occasionally, for 3 to 5 minutes.

Make ahead

Grate Emmentaler and Gruyère and combine in a bowl; refrigerate until needed.

Toast and chop almonds.

Serve with...

Cubes of crusty French bread, chunks of cinnamon buns or raisin bread, apples, steamed vegetables.

Emmentaler Fondue with Caramelized Shallots

Serves 4

Tip

Lavash is a type of crispy flatbread available at Middle Eastern markets or specialty food stores. While it cannot be speared and fondued in the traditional sense, it makes an excellent dipper (by hand) with this cheese fondue.

Make ahead

Grate Emmentaler and Gruyère and combine in a bowl; refrigerate until needed.

Slice shallots.

Serve with...

Cubes of French bread or fergasa bread, lavash (see tip, above), boiled shrimp, blanched vegetables.

6 oz	Emmentaler cheese, grated	175 g
6 oz	Gruyère cheese, grated	175 g
1 tbsp	all-purpose flour	15 mL
1 tbsp	butter	15 mL
1/3 cup	sliced shallots	75 mL
1 1/2 tsp	granulated sugar	7 mL
1/2 tsp	Worcestershire sauce	2 mL
2 tbsp	dry sherry	25 mL
1 cup	dry white wine	250 mL

1. In a bowl, combine Emmentaler, Gruyère and flour; mix well to coat cheese with flour. Set aside.

2. In a medium saucepan, melt butter over medium heat. Add shallots and sauté for 2 minutes or until starting to brown. Sprinkle with sugar; reduce heat to low and sauté for another 6 to 8 minutes or until shallots are caramelized. Add Worcestershire sauce and sherry. Simmer for 1 minute or until liquid evaporates. Remove from heat.

3. In a large saucepan, bring white wine to a simmer over medium heat. Stir in shallot mixture. Reduce heat to medium-low.

4. Add cheese mixture by handfuls to wine mixture, stirring constantly after each addition with a wooden spoon in a figure-eight motion until cheese is melted. Transfer to fondue pot and serve immediately.

Emmentaler-Gruyère Fondue with Roasted Garlic

6 oz	Emmentaler cheese, grated	175 g
6 oz	Gruyère cheese, grated	175 g
2 tbsp	kirsch (dry cherry schnapps)	25 mL
1 tbsp	cornstarch	15 mL
1 cup	dry white wine, divided	250 mL
½ tsp	ground nutmeg	2 mL
2	roasted garlic cloves, minced	2

1. In a bowl, combine Emmentaler and Gruyère. Set aside.

2. In a small bowl, whisk together kirsch and cornstarch until dissolved. Set aside.

3. In a large saucepan over medium heat, bring ¾ cup (175 mL) of the wine to a simmer. Reduce heat to medium-low. Add cheese mixture by handfuls to saucepan, whisking constantly after each addition in a figure-eight motion until cheese is almost all melted. Add nutmeg and kirsch mixture; stir until blended and cheese is completely melted.

4. Stir in as much of the remaining wine as necessary to give the mixture a creamy consistency. Transfer to fondue pot and stir in roasted garlic. Serve immediately.

Serves 4

Tip

To roast garlic: Divide 1 head of garlic into cloves. Place unpeeled cloves (as many as desired) onto baking sheet sprayed with olive oil cooking spray. Bake in 375°F (190°C) oven for about 25 minutes, turning once after 15 minutes. Garlic cloves should be tender. Remove from oven, cool slightly, peel and mince. Set aside. If garlic is too tender, just squeeze out roasted garlic cloves from skins and use as required.

Make ahead

Grate Emmentaler and Gruyère and combine in a bowl; refrigerate until needed.

Roast garlic as directed (see tip, above).

Serve with...
Cubes of French bread, steamed new potatoes, rye bread chunks, breadsticks (for dipping).

Edam Tarragon Fondue

Edam blends well with the tarragon and grainy mustard.

Tip
Like many cheese fondues, this one is complemented by a glass of dry red wine. Serve Cabernet Sauvignon for a fantastic pairing of flavors.

Make ahead
Grate Emmentaler and Edam and combine in a bowl; refrigerate until needed.

Chop tarragon.

Serve with...
Cubes of French bread or challah, boiled new potatoes, bread sticks, gherkins.

8 oz	Emmentaler cheese, grated	250 g
4 oz	Edam cheese, grated	125 g
1 tbsp	cornstarch	15 mL
1	clove garlic, halved	1
¾ cup	white wine	175 mL
2 tsp	freshly squeezed lemon juice	10 mL
1 tbsp	grainy or Dijon mustard	15 mL
1 tbsp	chopped fresh tarragon (or 1 tsp/5 mL dried)	15 mL

1. In a bowl, combine Emmentaler, Edam and cornstarch; mix well to coat cheese with cornstarch. Set aside.

2. Rub the inside of a large saucepan with cut sides of garlic. Discard garlic. Add wine and lemon juice; bring to a simmer over medium heat. Reduce heat to medium-low.

3. Stir in grainy mustard. Add cheese mixture by handfuls to saucepan, stirring constantly after each addition with a wooden spoon in a figure-eight motion until cheese is melted.

4. Stir in tarragon; mix well. Transfer to fondue pot and serve immediately.

Swiss Cheese and Black Olive Fondue

8 oz	Emmentaler cheese, grated	250 g
8 oz	Gruyère cheese, grated	250 g
1½ tbsp	all-purpose flour	22 mL
1	clove garlic, halved	1
1¼ cups	dry white wine	300 mL
3 tbsp	black olives, chopped	45 mL

1. In a bowl, combine Emmentaler, Gruyère and flour; mix well to coat cheese with flour. Set aside.

2. Rub the inside of a large saucepan with cut sides of garlic. Discard garlic. Add wine and bring to a simmer over medium heat. Reduce heat to medium-low.

3. Add cheese mixture by handfuls to saucepan, whisking constantly after each addition in a figure-eight motion until cheese is melted. Remove from heat. Stir in olives. Transfer to fondue pot and serve immediately.

Serves 4 as a main course or 6 as an appetizer

Tips
Add more olives for a stronger olive flavor.

Remember to stir cheese constantly during the fondue to prevent scorching.

Make ahead
Grate Emmentaler and Gruyère and combine in a bowl; refrigerate until needed.

Chop olives.

Serve with...
Focaccia wedges, French bread or sourdough cubes, boiled new potatoes, blanched red peppers, zucchini rounds, mushrooms, broccoli florets.

Maple Cheese Fondue

This is a very sweet fondue and can easily be served as a dessert. It's magnificent served with Granny Smith apple wedges.

Make ahead

Grate Emmentaler and Gruyère and combine in a bowl; refrigerate until needed.

Serve with...

Granny Smith apple wedges, cubes of French bread and sourdough bread.

8 oz	Emmentaler cheese, grated	250 g
4 oz	Gruyère cheese, grated	125 g
1 tbsp	cornstarch	15 mL
1 cup	dry white wine	250 mL
½ cup	pure maple syrup	125 mL
2 oz	rye whisky	60 mL

1. In a bowl, combine Emmentaler, Gruyère and cornstarch; mix well to coat cheese with cornstarch. Set aside.

2. In a large saucepan, combine wine, maple syrup and rye; bring to a simmer over medium heat. Reduce heat to medium-low.

3. Add cheese mixture by handfuls to saucepan, stirring constantly after each addition with a wooden spoon in a figure-eight motion until cheese is melted. Transfer to fondue pot and serve immediately.

Double-Smoked Jarlsberg and Almond Fondue

8 oz	Jarlsberg cheese, grated	250 g
4 oz	Gruyère cheese, grated	125 g
1 tbsp	all-purpose flour	15 mL
1	clove garlic, halved	1
1 cup	dry white wine	250 mL
2 tsp	freshly squeezed lemon juice	10 mL
½ tsp	smoked paprika	2 mL
¼ cup	finely chopped smoked almonds	50 mL

1. In a bowl, combine Jarlsberg, Gruyère and flour; mix well to coat cheese with flour. Set aside.

2. Rub the inside of a large saucepan with cut sides of garlic. Discard garlic. Add wine and lemon juice; bring to a simmer over medium heat. Reduce heat to medium-low.

3. Add cheese mixture by handfuls to saucepan, stirring constantly after each addition with a wooden spoon in a figure-eight motion until cheese is melted.

4. Stir in smoked paprika; mix well. Transfer to fondue pot and garnish with almonds. Serve immediately.

Serves 4

Smoked almonds provide an enticing smoky flavor, especially when paired with the intensity of smoked paprika.

Tip
Smoked paprika (pimentón) is produced in Spain and is available at specialty shops. It can be sweet, bittersweet or hot, depending on the pepper that is smoked. Use sweet or hot smoked paprika to complement this fondue.

Make ahead
Grate Jarlsberg and Gruyère and combine in a bowl; refrigerate until needed.

Chop almonds so they are ready to go.

Serve with...
Cubes of French bread, dark rye, Icelandic brown bread or raisin bread.

Jarlsberg and Chive Fondue

Serves 4

Nutty Jarlsberg boasts a robust flavor that pairs well with a burst of chives — especially in the spring, as chives come into season.

Make ahead

Grate Jarlsberg and Emmentaler and combine in a bowl; refrigerate until needed.

Chop chives.

Serve with...

Cubes of French bread, breadsticks, boiled new potatoes, blanched asparagus.

8 oz	Jarlsberg cheese, grated	250 g
4 oz	Emmentaler cheese, grated	125 g
1 tbsp	cornstarch	15 mL
1	shallot, minced	1
¾ cup	dry white wine	175 mL
2 tsp	freshly squeezed lemon juice	10 mL
⅓ cup	chopped fresh chives	75 mL

1. In a bowl, combine Jarlsberg, Emmentaler and cornstarch; mix well to coat cheese with cornstarch. Set aside.

2. In a large saucepan, combine shallot, white wine and lemon juice; bring to a simmer over medium heat. Reduce heat to medium-low.

3. Add cheese mixture by handfuls to saucepan, stirring constantly after each addition with a wooden spoon in a figure-eight motion until cheese is melted. Transfer to fondue pot and stir in chives. Serve immediately.

Oka Cheese Fondue

12 oz	Oka cheese (see tip, at right), grated	375 mL
1 tbsp	cornstarch	15 mL
1	clove garlic, halved	1
¾ cup	Canadian dry white wine	175 mL
2 tsp	freshly squeezed lemon juice	10 mL

1. In a bowl, combine Oka cheese and cornstarch; mix well to coat cheese with cornstarch. Set aside.

2. Rub the inside of a large saucepan with cut sides of garlic. Discard garlic. Add wine and lemon juice; bring to a simmer over medium heat. Reduce heat to medium-low.

3. Add cheese mixture by handfuls to saucepan, stirring constantly after each addition with a wooden spoon in a figure-eight motion until cheese is melted. Transfer to fondue pot and serve immediately.

Serves 4

Oka cheese is a semi-soft cheese with a complex flavor: it is buttery, yet also boasts fruit and nut undertones. Creamy Oka cheese melts beautifully. It was first produced in the 19th century by Trappist monks in Quebec. To this day, it is still made in Quebec; fortunately, it's available elsewhere.

Tip
In place of Oka, you can use Vacherin or Cantonnier cheese.

Make ahead
Grate Oka and refrigerate until needed.

Serve with...
Cubes of French or Italian bread, chunks of cinnamon buns or croissants, boiled mini potatoes, marinated mushrooms, blanched broccoli florets.

Quebec Cheese Fondue

Sir Laurier d'Arthabaska is a soft refined cheese with a washed rind that is produced in the Bois-Francs region of Quebec and available in specialty cheese shops. Known for its distinctive aroma and flavor, the cheese was named after Sir Wilfrid Laurier, the first French-Canadian Prime Minister of Canada (1896–1911).

Tip

If you can't find Sir Laurier d'Arthabaska special cheese, substitute a triple-cream Brie or Camembert, trimmed and cubed.

Make ahead

Trim and cube Sir Laurier d'Arthabaska cheese and grate Gruyère and Emmentaler. Combine in a bowl and refrigerate until needed.

Serve with...

Cubes of French baguette, sourdough bread or focaccia, blanched broccoli florets.

4 oz	Sir Laurier d'Arthabaska cheese (see tip, at left), trimmed and cubed	125 g
4 oz	Gruyère cheese, grated	125 g
2 oz	Emmentaler cheese, grated	60 g
1 tbsp	cornstarch	15 mL
1	clove garlic, halved	1
¾ cup	dry white wine	175 mL
¼ cup	whipping (35%) cream	50 mL
2 tsp	freshly squeezed lemon juice	10 mL

1. In a bowl, combine Sir Laurier d'Arthabaska, Gruyère, Emmentaler and cornstarch; mix well to coat cheese with cornstarch. Set aside.

2. Rub the inside of a large saucepan with cut sides of garlic. Discard garlic. Add wine and bring to a simmer over medium heat. Reduce heat to medium-low. Add whipping cream and simmer for 3 minutes or until smooth.

3. Add cheese mixture by handfuls to saucepan, stirring constantly after each addition with a wooden spoon in a figure-eight motion until cheese is melted. (Be sure cheese is thoroughly melted after each addition.)

4. When cheese is completely melted, stir in lemon juice. Transfer to fondue pot and serve immediately.

Three-Cheese and Porcini Fondue

½ oz	dried porcini mushrooms	15 g
½ cup	dry white wine	125 mL
1	clove garlic, minced	1
¾ cup	chopped fresh mushrooms (button or wild varieties)	175 mL
4 oz	Cantonnier (or Gouda or Oka) cheese, cubed	125 g
4 oz	Emmentaler cheese, grated	125 g
4 oz	Gruyère cheese, grated	125 g

1. In a measuring cup, cover dried mushrooms with 1 cup (250 mL) boiling water; soak for 15 minutes. Drain mushrooms, reserving liquid; chop and set aside.

2. In a large saucepan, bring wine to a simmer over medium heat. Add minced garlic, fresh mushrooms and reserved soaking liquid; reduce heat and simmer for 3 minutes.

3. Add cheese by handfuls to saucepan, stirring constantly after each addition with a wooden spoon in a figure-eight motion until the cheese is melted.

4. Stir in chopped reconstituted mushrooms until mixed through. Transfer to fondue pot and serve immediately.

Serves 4

Once dried, wild mushrooms take on a more intense flavor and aroma. Experiment with different varieties of dried mushrooms — for example, mixing porcini with dried chanterelles and morels.

Tips
For an earthier taste, substitute fresh wild mushrooms for the mushrooms.

To reconstitute dried wild mushrooms, cover with boiling water and soak for 15 minutes; drain, reserving liquid, and use as desired.

Cantonnier is a specialty of Canadian cheesemakers. It is creamy, with a soft texture, nutty flavor and rich aroma.

Make ahead
Cube Cantonnier and grate Emmentaler and Gruyère. Combine in a bowl and refrigerate until needed.

Serve with...
Cubes of crusty French, Italian or sourdough bread.

Bacon Cheese Fondue

Serves 4

Tips
Always use old Cheddar — not mild or medium — for a stronger flavor.

Cool the bacon completely before crumbling.

If fondue appears too thick, warm 1 to 2 tbsp (15 to 25 mL) milk and gently stir into saucepan before transferring to fondue pot.

The cheese and bacon in this recipe are both quite salty, so taste before seasoning.

Make ahead
Fry the bacon, let cool and then crumble.

Grate Gruyère and Cheddar and combine in a bowl; refrigerate until needed.

Serve with...
English muffins (cut into wedges), bagels in chunks or French bread.

6	slices bacon	6
1 cup	sour cream	250 mL
8 oz	Gruyère cheese, grated	250 g
4 oz	old Cheddar cheese, grated	125 g
	Salt and freshly ground black pepper to taste	
Pinch	ground nutmeg	Pinch
½ tsp	Worcestershire sauce	2 mL
¼ tsp	dry mustard	1 mL

1. In a skillet, fry bacon until crisp. Drain bacon on a paper towel and allow to cool; crumble and set aside.

2. In a large saucepan, heat sour cream over low heat. Meanwhile, in a bowl, combine Gruyère and Cheddar until well mixed.

3. Add cheese by handfuls to saucepan, stirring constantly after each addition with a wooden spoon in a figure-eight motion until the cheese is melted.

4. Add Worcestershire and dry mustard; mix well. Stir in salt, pepper and nutmeg. Transfer to fondue pot. Stir in crumbled bacon.

Cheddar and Pimiento Fondue

8 oz	old Cheddar cheese, grated	250 g
4 oz	Gruyère cheese, grated	125 g
1 tbsp	all-purpose flour	15 mL
½ cup	lager beer, at room temperature	125 mL
2 tsp	freshly squeezed lemon juice	10 mL
½ tsp	Worcestershire sauce	2 mL
½ tsp	dry mustard	2 mL
¼ cup	chopped drained pimientos	50 mL

1. In a bowl, combine Cheddar, Gruyère and flour; mix well to coat cheese with flour. Set aside.

2. In a large saucepan, combine beer and lemon juice; bring to a simmer over medium heat. Reduce heat to medium-low.

3. Add cheese mixture by handfuls to saucepan, stirring constantly after each addition with a wooden spoon in a figure-eight motion until cheese is melted.

4. Add Worcestershire and dry mustard, stirring well. Transfer to fondue pot. Add pimiento. Mix well and serve.

Serves 4

Tip
Pimiento, a Spanish sweet pepper, is often used to stuff olives and add color to various dishes. You can replace the pimiento with roasted red pepper, if desired.

Make ahead

Grate Cheddar and Gruyère and combine in a bowl; refrigerate until needed.

Chop drained pimientos or roast red peppers.

Serve with...
Toasted French bread cubes, breadsticks, marinated artichoke hearts, pitted olives.

Cheddar and Spinach Fondue

Processed Cheddar helps to create a creamy fondue — the perfect complement to vitamin-packed spinach.

Make ahead

Cube processed Cheddar and grate old Cheddar. Combine in a bowl and refrigerate until ready to use.

Blanch spinach.

Serve with...

Cubes of French bread, lightly toasted English muffin wedges, lightly toasted bagel chunks, Granny Smith apple sections.

8 oz	processed Cheddar cheese block, cubed	250 g
4 oz	old Cheddar cheese, grated	125 g
1 tbsp	all-purpose flour	15 mL
1 cup	beer	250 mL
1 tbsp	grainy or Dijon mustard	15 mL
Pinch	ground nutmeg	Pinch
	Freshly ground black pepper to taste	
2 cups	chopped spinach, blanched for 1 minute and squeezed dry	250 mL

1. In a bowl, combine processed Cheddar, old Cheddar and flour; mix well to coat cheese with flour.

2. In a large saucepan, bring beer to a simmer over medium heat. Reduce heat to medium-low.

3. Add cheese mixture by handfuls to saucepan, stirring constantly after each addition with a wooden spoon in a figure-eight motion until cheese is melted.

4. Stir in mustard; mix well. Sprinkle with nutmeg and pepper, then stir in spinach. Transfer to fondue pot and serve immediately.

Cheddar Cheese and Beer Fondue

6 oz	Monterey Jack cheese, grated	175 g
4 oz	Gruyère cheese, grated	125 g
4 oz	sharp processed Cheddar cheese, grated	125 g
1½ tbsp	all-purpose flour	22 mL
1 cup	lager beer, at room temperature	250 mL
1 tsp	dry mustard	5 mL

1. In a bowl, combine Monterey Jack, Gruyère, sharp Cheddar and flour; mix well to coat cheese with flour. Set aside.

2. In a large saucepan, bring beer to a simmer over medium heat. Reduce heat to medium-low.

3. Add cheese mixture by handfuls to saucepan, stirring constantly after each addition with a wooden spoon in a figure-eight motion until cheese is melted.

4. When cheese is nearly all melted, stir in dry mustard, mixing well. Transfer to fondue pot and serve immediately.

Serves 4

Sharp processed Cheddar is intensely flavorful and melts wonderfully.

Tips

Allow cold beer to warm to room temperature before using. Be sure beer is not too carbonated, since this will affect the quality of the fondue.

Look for sharp processed cheddar in the dairy section of the supermarket alongside other processed cheese. Keep refrigerated until ready to grate.

For extra zing, stir in 1 tsp (5 mL) Worcestershire sauce and a few drops of hot pepper sauce when cheese is nearly melted; mix well.

Make ahead

Grate Monterey Jack, Gruyère and Cheddar. Combine in a bowl and refrigerate until needed.

Serve with...

Garlic French bread cubes, cherry or grape tomatoes, blanched asparagus, green beans.

Quick Cheese Fondue

This is an easy fondue, ideal for teenage cooks.

Tips

Sharp processed Cheddar cheese is found in the refrigerator section of the supermarket. Its strong flavor makes it a wonderful addition to fondues. Grate directly from refrigerator, while still cold.

If fondue is too thin, gradually stir in an additional 1 tsp (5 mL) flour. If too thick, warm 1/4 cup (50 mL) unsweetened apple cider and stir a little bit at a time into saucepan until desired consistency is reached.

Use apple juice in place of apple cider if desired.

Make ahead

Grate cheeses and refrigerate until needed.

Serve with...

Cubes of white rolls, blanched asparagus, broccoli, carrot sticks, zucchini, mushrooms, yellow and red pepper strips, cooked large rotini.

6 oz	old Cheddar cheese, grated	175 g
2 oz	sharp processed Cheddar cheese, grated	60 g
1	clove garlic, halved	1
1/2 cup	unsweetened apple cider	125 mL
1	can (10 oz/284 mL) condensed cheese soup	1
1/4 tsp	Worcestershire sauce	1 mL
	Freshly ground black pepper to taste	

1. In a bowl, combine old Cheddar and sharp Cheddar cheese. Set aside.

2. Rub the inside of a large saucepan with cut sides of garlic. Discard garlic. Add cider and bring to a simmer over medium heat. Stir in cheese soup; mix until thoroughly blended.

3. Without reducing heat, add cheese mixture by handfuls to saucepan, stirring constantly after each addition until cheese is melted and smooth. Stir in Worcestershire. Season to taste with pepper. Transfer to fondue pot and serve immediately.

Curry Cheese Fondue

8 oz	cold-pack sharp Cheddar cheese, grated	250 g
1	package (8 oz/250 g) cream cheese, cubed	1
1	clove garlic, halved	1
½ cup	dry white wine	125 mL
2 tsp	curry powder	10 mL

1. In a bowl, combine Cheddar cheese and cream cheese. Set aside.

2. Rub the inside of a large saucepan with cut sides of garlic. Discard garlic. Add wine; bring to a simmer over medium heat. Reduce heat to medium-low.

3. Add cheese by handfuls to saucepan, stirring constantly after each addition with a wooden spoon in a figure-eight motion until cheese is melted.

4. Stir in curry powder; mix well. Transfer to fondue pot and serve immediately.

Serves 6

This recipe is perfect for entertaining.

Tips
Cold-pack sharp Cheddar is sold in plastic containers alongside other processed cheeses. It has an intense flavor and melts marvelously. Always grate directly from the refrigerator.

You can use light cream cheese in this recipe with great results.

For added depth, stir in 2 tbsp (25 mL) hot mango chutney with the curry powder and, just before serving, sprinkle with 2 tbsp (25 mL) each sliced toasted almonds and minced green onions.

Make ahead
Grate Cheddar and cube cream cheese. Combine in a bowl and refrigerate until ready to use.

Serve with...
Cubes of French bread, rice crackers, wedges of Indian naan bread, boiled mini potatoes, pearl onions, blanched cauliflower florets.

Quick Curry, Cheese and Mushroom Fondue

Serves 4		

Tips

Curry powder is a blend of many spices, including coriander, cumin and fennel seeds, black peppercorns, fenugreek seeds, cinnamon, cardamom pods, cloves, hot chilies, dried curry leaves and turmeric.

Make sure you replenish your curry powder after a few months or it will have lost its fragrance and flavor.

Add more curry powder at the end of cooking if desired.

Try replacing mushrooms with cremini mushrooms. They have a firmer texture and an earthier flavor.

Make ahead

Grate cheese and chop mushrooms.

Serve with...

Wedges of Indian naan bread, blanched broccoli and cauliflower, asparagus, cherry tomatoes, canned chickpeas (spear one chickpea on each tine of the fondue fork).

2 tbsp	butter, divided	25 mL
½ cup	chopped mushrooms	125 mL
1	clove garlic, minced	1
1	green onion (white part only), minced	1
1 tsp	curry powder	5 mL
½	can (10 oz/284 mL) cream of mushroom soup	½
¼ cup	milk	50 mL
8 oz	old Cheddar cheese, grated	250 g

1. In a small saucepan, melt 1 tbsp (15 mL) of the butter over medium heat. Add mushrooms and sauté for about 2 minutes or until browned. Set aside.

2. In another larger saucepan, melt remaining 1 tbsp (15 mL) butter over medium heat. Add garlic, green onions and curry powder; sauté for about 2 minutes or until browned. Stir in mushroom soup and milk; continue to stir until well blended and heated through.

3. Without reducing heat, add cheese mixture by handfuls to saucepan, stirring constantly after each addition with a wooden spoon in a figure-eight motion until cheese is melted. Stir in reserved sautéed mushrooms. Transfer to fondue pot and serve immediately

Rarebit-Style Fondue

2 tbsp	butter	25 mL
1 cup	milk	250 mL
8 oz	processed cheese block, cubed	250 g
	Salt and freshly ground black pepper to taste	
½ tsp	Worcestershire sauce	2 mL
¼ tsp	dry mustard	1 mL
Pinch	cayenne pepper	Pinch
2	egg yolks, beaten	
1 tbsp	minced green onion (white part only)	15 mL

1. In a large saucepan over medium heat, stir together butter and milk. Heat until hot (but not boiling). Reduce heat to medium-low.

2. Add cheese by handfuls to saucepan, stirring constantly after each addition with wooden spoon in a figure-eight motion until cheese is melted. Season to taste with salt and pepper. Stir in Worcestershire, dry mustard and cayenne pepper.

3. Pour ½ cup (125 mL) of the cheese sauce into a large measuring cup. Whisk in egg yolks and return mixture to saucepan. Increase heat to medium and cook, stirring, for 4 minutes or until thickened.

4. Transfer to fondue pot and garnish with green onions. Serve immediately.

Serves 4

Welsh rarebit (sometimes mistakenly called rabbit) sauce is basically a spicy white sauce with cheese, traditionally served on toast. It makes an excellent brunch fondue.

Tip
This recipe features a lovely smooth texture, but it will thicken up in the heat of the fondue pot. Be sure to stir continuously to avoid scorching.

Variation
Fry 4 slices of bacon, let cool and crumble. Top Rarebit-Style Fondue with crumbled bacon just before serving.

Make ahead
Cube cheese and refrigerate until needed.

Fry bacon, if using.

Serve with...
Lightly toasted English muffin wedges, lightly toasted bagel chunks, baked potato puffs.

White Cheddar and Green Peppercorn Fondue

The combination of old white Cheddar (the older the better!), Gruyère and green peppercorns creates an irresistible taste sensation.

Tip
Use a mortar and pestle instead of a pepper grinder to crush the peppercorns — this will give them a more pronounced presence in the fondue.

Make ahead
Grate Cheddar and Gruyère and combine in a bowl; refrigerate until needed.

Serve with...
Cubes of French or sourdough bread, lightly toasted pita bread wedges, pretzels, gherkins, pearl onions.

8 oz	old white Cheddar cheese, grated	250 g
4 oz	Gruyère cheese, grated	125 g
1 tbsp	all-purpose flour	15 mL
1	clove garlic, halved	1
½ cup	beer, at room temperature	125 mL
2 tsp	freshly squeezed lime juice	10 mL
1 tbsp	grainy mustard	15 mL
	Green peppercorns, coarsely ground	

1. In a bowl, combine Cheddar, Gruyère and flour; mix well to coat cheese with flour. Set aside.

2. Rub the inside of a large saucepan with cut sides of garlic. Discard garlic. Add beer and lime juice; bring to a simmer over medium heat. Reduce heat to medium-low.

3. Add cheese by handfuls to saucepan, stirring constantly after each addition with a wooden spoon in a figure-eight motion until cheese is melted.

4. Stir in grainy mustard; mix well. Transfer to fondue pot and sprinkle with peppercorns. Serve immediately.

Emmentaler-Gruyère Fondue
with Roasted Garlic (page 31)

Swiss Cheese and Black Olive Fondue (page 33)

Cheddar and Spinach Fondue (page 42)

Spicy Mexican Fondue (page 50)

Child-Friendly Mexican Fondue

10 oz	old Cheddar cheese, grated	300 g
5 oz	sharp processed Cheddar cheese, grated	150 g
3 tbsp	cornstarch	45 mL
1 cup	unsweetened apple cider	250 mL
2 tsp	freshly squeezed lime juice	10 mL
1 tbsp	mild salsa	15 mL
2 tbsp	chopped fresh cilantro	25 mL

1. In a bowl, combine old Cheddar, sharp Cheddar and cornstarch; mix well to coat cheese with cornstarch. Set aside.

2. In the top of double boiler set over simmering (not boiling) water, combine apple cider and lime juice; bring to a simmer.

3. Add cheese mixture by handfuls to double boiler, stirring constantly after each addition with a wooden spoon in a figure-eight motion until cheese is melted.

4. Stir in salsa, mixing well. Transfer to fondue pot and garnish with cilantro. Serve immediately.

Serves 4

Tips
For a spicier fondue, use hot instead of mild salsa, or stir in 1 tbsp (15 mL) chopped pickled jalapeños to the cheese just before transferring to fondue pot.

Sharp processed Cheddar cheese is found in the refrigerator section of the supermarket. Its strong flavor makes it a wonderful addition to fondues. Grate directly from refrigerator, while still cold.

Make ahead
Grate old and processed Cheddar and combine in a bowl; refrigerate until needed.

Wash, dry and chop cilantro.

Serve with...
Taco chips, cubes of cornbread and pumpernickel.

Spicy Mexican Fondue

Tips

Ancho chilies are dried poblanos. They are available at Latin markets and specialty food stores. If ancho chilies are unavailable, use chopped fresh serrano or jalapeño pepper. Increase the quantity of fresh chilies according to taste.

To reconstitute ancho chilies, soak in warm water for 30 minutes. Drain, remove seeds and mince.

Grate sharp processed Cheddar directly from refrigerator, while still cold.

Make ahead

Grate Monterey Jack, Gruyère and Cheddar. Combine in a bowl and refrigerate until needed.

Wash and chop cilantro.

Serve with...

Taco chips, pumpernickel, rye bread, cooked shrimp or cooked chicken pieces.

6 oz	Monterey Jack cheese, grated	175 g
4 oz	Gruyère cheese, grated	125 g
4 oz	sharp processed Cheddar cheese, grated	125 g
1 tbsp	cornstarch	15 mL
1 cup	lager beer, at room temperature	250 mL
1 tbsp	freshly squeezed lime juice	15 mL
1 tsp	chopped seeded ancho chilies	5 mL
2 tbsp	chopped fresh cilantro	25 mL

1. In a bowl, combine Monterey Jack, Gruyère, sharp Cheddar and cornstarch; mix well to coat cheese with cornstarch. Set aside.

2. In a large saucepan, combine beer and lime juice; bring to a simmer over medium heat. Reduce heat to medium-low.

3. Add cheese mixture by handfuls to saucepan, stirring constantly after each addition with a wooden spoon in a figure-eight motion until cheese is melted.

4. Stir in ancho chilies, mixing well. Transfer to fondue pot and garnish with cilantro. Serve immediately.

Monterey Jack and Chipotle Fondue

8 oz	Gruyère cheese, grated	250 g
4 oz	Monterey Jack cheese, grated	125 g
1 tbsp	cornstarch	15 mL
1	clove garlic, halved	1
½ cup	Mexican beer (such as Corona)	125 mL
1 tbsp	freshly squeezed lime juice	15 mL
1 tbsp	finely minced chipotle chilies in adobo sauce (see tips, at right)	15 mL

1. In a bowl, combine Gruyère, Monterey Jack and cornstarch; mix well to coat cheese with cornstarch. Set aside.

2. Rub the inside of a large saucepan with cut sides of garlic. Discard garlic. Add beer and lime juice; bring to a simmer over medium heat. Reduce heat to medium-low.

3. Add cheese mixture by handfuls to saucepan, stirring constantly after each addition with a wooden spoon in a figure-eight motion until cheese is melted.

4. Stir in chilies in adobo sauce; mix well. Transfer to fondue pot and serve immediately.

Serves 4

Tips
Chipotle chilies are smoked and dried cherry-red ripe jalapeños. They offer a unique piquant, smoky, sweet flavor. Look for canned chipotle chilies in a tomato adobo sauce, available at Latin markets and specialty food stores.

If you prefer a milder flavor, reduce the amount of chipotles.

When you add the chipotles, you may also add 1 green onion, minced, or 2 tbsp (25 mL) chopped fresh cilantro.

Make ahead
Grate Gruyère and Monterey Jack and combine in a bowl; refrigerate until needed.

Mince chipotle chilies (and green onion, if using).

Serve with...
Tortilla chips, cubes of crusty French bread or sourdough bread, cooked shrimp, jicama sticks, cherry tomatoes.

Creamed Corn Fondue with Chipotle Chilies

Processed cheese block is great for melting and adds creaminess to many fondues.

Tip
Chipotle chilies are smoked and dried cherry-red ripe jalapeños. Look for canned chipotle chilies in a tomato adobo sauce. If you prefer a milder flavor, reduce the amount of chipotle chilies. They are available in Latin markets and specialty food stores and offer a uniquely piquant, smoky-sweet flavor.

Make ahead
Grate Emmentaler and Gruyère and cube processed cheese. Combine in a bowl and refrigerate until needed.

Chop green onions and chipotle chilies.

Serve with...
Whole-grain bread cubes, tortilla shells (rolled and sliced in rounds for dipping), fresh jicama and celery sticks.

4 oz	Emmentaler cheese, grated	125 g
4 oz	Gruyère cheese, grated	125 g
4 oz	processed cheese block, cubed	125 g
1 tbsp	cornstarch	15 mL
1 tbsp	butter	15 mL
2 tbsp	finely chopped green onions	25 mL
1 cup	dry white wine	250 mL
Pinch	salt	Pinch
Pinch	cayenne pepper	Pinch
½ cup	creamed corn	125 mL
1 tbsp	chopped chipotle chilies (in adobo sauce, see tip, at left)	15 mL

1. In a bowl, combine Emmentaler, Gruyère, processed cheese and cornstarch; mix well to coat cheese with cornstarch. Set aside.

2. In a large saucepan, melt butter over medium heat. Add green onions and sauté until softened. Stir in white wine; bring to a simmer. Reduce heat to medium-low.

3. Add cheese mixture by handfuls to saucepan, stirring constantly after each addition with a wooden spoon in a figure-eight motion until cheese is melted.

4. Remove from heat and season with salt and cayenne pepper. Stir in creamed corn and chipotle chilies. Transfer to fondue pot and serve immediately.

Jack Pepper Cheese Fondue

6 oz	Friulano cheese, grated	175 g
6 oz	Monterey Jack jalapeño pepper cheese, grated	175 g
1 tbsp	all-purpose flour	15 mL
1	clove garlic, halved	1
½ cup	lager beer, at room temperature	125 mL
1 tbsp	freshly squeezed lime juice	15 mL

1. In a bowl, combine Friulano, Monterey Jack and flour; mix well to coat cheese with flour. Set aside.

2. Rub the inside of a large saucepan with cut sides of garlic. Discard garlic. Add beer and lime juice; bring to a simmer over medium heat. Reduce heat to medium low.

3. Add cheese mixture by handfuls to saucepan, stirring constantly with a wooden spoon in a figure-eight motion until cheese is melted. Transfer to fondue pot and serve immediately.

Monterey Jack pairs well with any kind of chili. Serve this fondue with chili con carne, a salad and crusty bread for dipping, and you have an excellent main course.

Tips
Monterey Jack is a true North American cheese, dating back to the early 1890s. It is a firm, creamy cheese with wonderful melting properties. You can find Monterey Jack (sometimes simply called Jack) seasoned with garlic, dill and other ingredients — so feel free to experiment with these different flavors.

Friulano, named after the Italian district of Friuli, is a firm cheese with a mildly milky aroma and taste. It becomes nuttier and more acidulous with age.

Make ahead
Grate Friulano and Monterey Jack and refrigerate until needed.

Serve with...
Cubes of French bread, toasted garlic bread, taco chips, cornbread.

Queso Fondido

Literally "melted cheese," queso fondido is a Mexican take on the Swiss fondue. In this version, roasted jalapeño and red bell peppers provide heat and a distinctive, wonderful flavor.

Tip

To roast peppers, place on a broiling pan and broil, turning often, for about 20 minutes or until peppers have blackened all over. Place peppers in a saucepan with a tight-fitting lid for 5 to 10 minutes. Peel and seed both peppers. Cut red pepper in half, chopping half of it and reserving the remainder for another use. Mince jalapeño pepper.

Make ahead

Grate cheeses and refrigerate until needed.

Roast jalapeño and red bell peppers.

Serve with...

Tortilla chips, lightly toasted pita bread wedges, sourdough bread cubes, chunks of dried pepperoni or salami, cherry tomatoes.

6 oz	Gruyère cheese, grated	175 g
4 oz	Monterey Jack cheese, grated	125 g
2 oz	Cheddar cheese, grated	60 g
1 tbsp	cornstarch	15 mL
1	clove garlic, halved	1
¾ cup	Mexican beer (such as Corona)	175 mL
1 tbsp	freshly squeezed lime juice	15 mL
1	jalapeño pepper, roasted (see tip, at left) and minced	1
½	red bell pepper, roasted (see tip, at left) and chopped	½
3	drops hot pepper sauce (optional)	3

1. In a bowl, combine Gruyère, Monterey Jack, Cheddar and cornstarch; mix well to coat cheese with cornstarch. Set aside.

2. Rub the inside of a large saucepan with cut sides of garlic. Discard garlic. Add beer and lime juice; bring to a simmer over medium heat. Reduce heat to medium-low.

3. Add cheese mixture by handfuls to saucepan, stirring constantly after each addition with a wooden spoon in a figure-eight motion until cheese is melted.

4. Stir in jalapeño and red peppers; mix well. Stir in hot pepper sauce, if using. Transfer to fondue pot and serve immediately.

Truffle Fondue

12 oz	Gruyère cheese, grated	375 g
4 oz	fontina cheese, grated	125 g
1 tbsp	cornstarch	15 mL
1	clove garlic, halved	1
1 cup	dry white wine	250 mL
2 tsp	white truffle oil (see tip, at right)	10 mL

1. In a bowl, combine Gruyère, fontina and cornstarch; mix well to coat cheese with cornstarch. Set aside.

2. Rub the inside of a large saucepan with cut sides of garlic. Discard garlic. Add white wine; bring to a simmer over medium heat. Reduce heat to medium-low.

3. Add cheese mixture by handfuls to saucepan, stirring constantly after each addition with a wooden spoon in a figure-eight motion until cheese is melted.

4. Stir in truffle oil; mix well. Transfer to fondue pot and serve immediately.

Serves 4 to 6

Tip
Found in gourmet food shops, truffle oil is the essence of truffles. It is an exquisite addition to this fondue, imparting an intense mushroom flavor. And its sensual aroma makes this the ideal fondue for Valentine's Day or any special occasion.

Make ahead
Grate Gruyère and fontina and combine in a bowl; refrigerate until needed.

Serve with...
Focaccia wedges, cubes of French bread or croissants, fergasa bread, cherry tomatoes, marinated mushrooms, blanched broccoli florets.

Italian Fondue

Tips

Fontina cheese has a slightly firm texture and a gentle bouquet — and it's ideal for melting. For superior results, try to find the genuine imported Italian fontina.

Mozzarella, known for its firm, elastic body, has a mild flavor that blends well with fontina and robust Parmigiano-Reggiano.

Make ahead

Grate fontina, mozzarella and Parmesan. Combine in a bowl and refrigerate until needed.

Serve with...

Crusty Italian bread cubes, grilled eggplant slices, blanched rapini, focaccia wedges, salami chunks, fresh mushrooms, cooked sausage chunks.

8 oz	fontina cheese, grated	250 g
2 oz	mozzarella cheese, grated	60 g
2 oz	Parmesan cheese (preferably Parmigiano-Reggiano), freshly grated	60 g
2 tsp	cornstarch	10 mL
1	clove garlic, halved	1
¾ cup	Italian dry white wine	175 mL
2 tsp	freshly squeezed lemon juice	10 mL

1. In a bowl, combine fontina, mozzarella, Parmesan and cornstarch; mix well to coat cheese with cornstarch. Set aside.

2. Rub the inside of a large saucepan with cut sides of garlic. Discard garlic. Add wine and lemon juice; bring to a simmer over medium heat. Reduce heat to medium-low.

3. Add cheese mixture by handfuls to saucepan, stirring constantly after each addition with a wooden spoon in a figure-eight motion until cheese is melted. Transfer to fondue pot and serve immediately.

Pizza Fondue

12 oz	mozzarella cheese, grated	375 g
1 oz	Parmesan cheese, freshly grated	30 g
1 tbsp	all-purpose flour	15 mL
2	cloves garlic, minced	2
¾ cup	dry white wine	175 mL
⅔ cup	drained canned diced tomatoes	150 mL
1 tbsp	balsamic vinegar	15 mL
1 tbsp	chopped fresh basil (or 1 tsp/5 mL dried)	15 mL
1 tbsp	chopped fresh oregano (or 1 tsp/5 mL dried)	15 mL

1. In a bowl, combine mozzarella, Parmesan and flour; mix well to coat cheese with flour. Set aside.

2. In a large saucepan, combine garlic and wine; bring to a simmer over medium heat. Reduce heat to medium-low.

3. Add cheese mixture by handfuls to saucepan, stirring constantly after each addition with a wooden spoon in a figure-eight motion until cheese is melted.

4. Stir in tomatoes, balsamic vinegar, basil and oregano; cook, stirring, until tomatoes are heated through, about 2 minutes. Transfer to fondue pot and serve immediately.

Serves 4

This fondue was a big hit with my teenage sons — they especially liked the addition of some different dippers to the cheese fondue experience.

Make ahead

Grate mozzarella and Parmesan and combine in a bowl; refrigerate until needed.

Serve with...

Cubes of crusty French bread, wedges of focaccia, breadsticks, pepperoni and salami cubes, cooked sausage chunks, bell pepper slices, mushrooms.

Roasted Red Pepper and Mozzarella Fondue

Tips

Red peppers can be roasted on the backyard barbecue, indoor grill or under the oven broiler.

To grill, place whole red peppers directly on barbecue or indoor grill over high heat. Turn peppers every few minutes, roasting for a total of about 5 to 10 minutes or until peppers are blackened and blistered.

For oven broiling, place on a broiling pan and broil, turning often, for about 20 minutes or until peppers have blackened all over.

Place peppers in a saucepan with a tight-fitting lid for 5 to 10 minutes, then peel, seed and use as desired.

Make ahead

Grate Gruyère and mozzarella and combine in a bowl; refrigerate until needed.

Roast red pepper.

Serve with...

Bread sticks, focaccia, pita bread triangles, steamed salmon chunks, cooked penne.

6 oz	Gruyère cheese, grated	175 g
6 oz	mozzarella cheese, grated	175 g
1 tbsp	all-purpose flour	15 mL
¾ cup	dry white wine	175 mL
1 tbsp	freshly squeezed lemon juice	15 mL
2	cloves garlic, minced	2
1 tbsp	kirsch (dry cherry schnapps)	15 mL
½	roasted red pepper (see tips, at left), minced	½

1. In a bowl, combine Gruyère, mozzarella and flour; mix well to coat cheese with flour. Set aside.

2. In a large saucepan, combine wine, lemon juice and garlic; bring to a simmer over medium heat. Reduce heat to medium-low.

3. Add cheese mixture by handfuls to saucepan, stirring constantly after each addition with a wooden spoon in a figure-eight motion until cheese is melted.

4. Remove from heat. Stir in kirsch and red pepper. Transfer to fondue pot and serve immediately.

Caraway Gouda Fondue

6 oz	Edam cheese, grated	175 g
6 oz	spiced Gouda cheese (with caraway seeds), grated	175 g
2 oz	Gruyère cheese, grated	60 g
2 tsp	cornstarch	10 mL
1	clove garlic, halved	1
⅔ cup	lager beer, at room temperature	150 mL
1 tsp	freshly squeezed lime juice	5 mL

1. In a bowl, combine Edam, spiced Gouda, Gruyère and cornstarch; mix well to coat cheese with cornstarch. Set aside.

2. Rub the inside of a large saucepan with cut sides of garlic. Discard garlic. Add beer and lime juice; bring to a simmer over medium heat. Reduce heat to medium-low.

3. Add cheese mixture by handfuls to saucepan, stirring constantly after each addition with a wooden spoon in a figure-eight motion until cheese is melted. Transfer to fondue pot and serve immediately.

Serves 4

Tip
With its malty, sweetish flavor, lager beer is best suited for fondue cooking. Other types tend to be too strong (stout, for example) or too acidic (such as hoppy, English-style ales).

Make ahead
Grate Edam, Gouda and Gruyère. Combine in a bowl and refrigerate until needed.

Serve with...
Cubes of French, dark rye, pumpernickel and multigrain bread, cucumber chunks, red and green pepper slices, pickled onions

Smoked Gouda Fondue

The smoked Gouda in this fondue is both unusual and delicious — a delight for anyone who loves the flavor of smoked foods.

Tip
If possible, use Gouda imported from Holland for best results.

Make ahead
Grate Gruyère and Gouda and combine in a bowl; refrigerate until needed.

Serve with...
Cubes of French bread, egg bread or light rye and your choice of blanched vegetables (see tip, page 61).

8 oz	Gruyère cheese, grated	250 g
4 oz	smoked Gouda cheese, grated	125 g
1 tbsp	all-purpose flour	15 mL
1	clove garlic, halved	1
¾ cup	dry white wine	175 mL
1½ tsp	freshly squeezed lemon juice	7 mL

1. In a bowl, combine Gruyère, smoked Gouda and flour; mix well to coat cheese with flour. Set aside.

2. Rub the inside of a large saucepan with cut sides of garlic. Discard garlic. Add wine and lemon juice; bring to a simmer over medium heat. Reduce heat to medium-low.

3. Add cheese mixture by handfuls to saucepan, stirring constantly after each addition with a wooden spoon in a figure-eight motion until cheese is melted. Transfer to fondue pot and serve immediately.

Blue Cheese Fondue

1	package (8 oz/250 g) cream cheese, at room temperature, cubed	1
4 oz	blue cheese, crumbled	125 g
1 tbsp	butter	15 mL
¼ cup	minced leeks (white and light green parts only)	50 mL
1	shallot, minced	1
⅔ cup	half-and-half (10%) cream	150 mL

1. In a bowl, combine cream cheese and blue cheese; mix well. Set aside.

2. In a large saucepan, melt butter over medium heat. Add leeks and shallot; sauté until softened. Stir in cream; heat through (do not boil). Reduce heat to medium-low.

3. Add cheese mixture in small amounts to saucepan, whisking constantly after each addition until melted. Transfer to fondue pot and serve immediately.

Serves 4

This creamy fondue offers a subtle hint of blue cheese.

Tips
Add a sprinkle of cayenne pepper for extra kick.

To blanch vegetables for the dippers, immerse in boiling water (uncovered) for about 5 minutes or until tender-crisp.

Make ahead
Cube cream cheese and crumble blue cheese. Combine in a bowl and refrigerate until ready to use.

Mince leeks and shallot.

Serve with...
Cubes of French bread, blanched vegetables (such as broccoli, asparagus and cauliflower), pear sections.

Roquefort Fondue with Caramelized Walnuts

Serves 4

Serve this fondue as a side dish to Classic Beef Bourguignonne (see page 78). Fondue beef in oil, then top with sensational blue cheese topping.

Tip

To caramelize walnuts, in a small skillet over medium heat, sauté ¼ cup (50 mL) chopped walnuts and 1 tbsp (15 mL) packed brown sugar until walnuts turn golden brown. Place on a sheet of foil to cool, then break apart.

Make ahead

Grate Emmentaler and crumble Roquefort. Combine in a bowl and refrigerate until ready to use.

Caramelize walnuts.

Serve with...

Cubes of French bread and multigrain baguette, fondued beef, boiled new potatoes, blanched vegetables (see tip, page 61), pear and apple wedges.

8 oz	Emmentaler cheese, grated	250 g
3½ oz	Roquefort cheese, crumbled	100 g
1 tbsp	all-purpose flour	15 mL
1 tbsp	butter	15 mL
2	shallots, minced	2
1	clove garlic, minced	1
½ cup	dry white wine	125 mL
1 tsp	freshly squeezed lemon juice	5 mL
¼ cup	caramelized walnuts (see tip, at left)	50 mL

1. In a bowl, combine Emmentaler, Roquefort and flour; mix well to coat cheese with flour. Set aside.

2. In a large saucepan, melt butter over medium heat. Add shallots and garlic; sauté until softened. Add wine and lemon juice; bring to a simmer over medium heat. Reduce heat to medium-low.

3. Add cheese mixture by handfuls to saucepan, stirring constantly after each addition with a wooden spoon in a figure-eight motion until cheese is melted.

4. Stir in caramelized walnuts; mix well. Transfer to fondue pot and serve immediately.

Cream Cheese and Crab Fondue

1	package (8 oz/250 g) cream cheese, at room temperature	1
1 cup	half-and-half (10%) cream, divided	250 mL
1 tbsp	butter	15 mL
2 tbsp	minced green onions	25 mL
1	clove garlic, minced	1
4 oz	blue cheese, crumbled	125 g
8 oz	crabmeat, flaked	250 g
2 tbsp	freshly squeezed lemon juice	25 mL
1/4 tsp	hot pepper sauce	1 mL

1. In a bowl, with an electric mixer, beat together softened cream cheese and 1/2 cup (125 mL) of the cream until smooth. Set aside.

2. In a large saucepan, melt butter over medium heat. Add green onions and garlic; sauté until softened. Stir in remaining 1/2 cup (125 mL) cream; cook until hot (not boiling). Reduce heat to simmer.

3. Add cream cheese mixture in small amounts to saucepan, whisking constantly after each addition. Add blue cheese, whisking constantly until melted.

4. Stir in crabmeat, lemon juice and hot pepper sauce. Mix well. Transfer to fondue pot and serve immediately.

Serves 4

Tips
If you can find it, use fresh crabmeat for the best flavor. Otherwise, use canned crabmeat.

Add more hot pepper sauce for extra zing.

To blanch vegetables, immerse in a pot of boiling water and cook, uncovered, for about 5 minutes or until tender-crisp. Refresh under cold water to stop cooking. Drain.

Make ahead
Beat cream cheese with half-and-half and set aside.

Chop green onions and mince garlic.

If using canned crabmeat, drain and remove cartilage in advance.

Serve with...
Sourdough bread cubes, blanched vegetables (such as broccoli and asparagus), slices of fresh red and green bell peppers.

Smoked Salmon and Cream Cheese Fondue

This fabulous lox and cream cheese fondue is ideal for a brunch or as an appetizer with white wine — be sure to serve it with bagel chunks.

Tips

If using frozen smoked salmon, be sure to thaw it thoroughly before slicing. The pieces should be about 1 inch (2.5 cm).

Warm bagels in toaster oven on medium heat for about 5 minutes, then cut into thick chunks for dippers.

Use 2 tbsp (25 mL) chopped fresh chives in place of the green onions.

Serve with capers as garnish.

Make ahead

Cube cheeses and refrigerate until needed.

Slice smoked salmon and refrigerate until needed.

Serve with...

Bagel chunks, cubes of pumpernickel and rye bread, breadsticks, lightly toasted English muffin wedges, lightly toasted pita bread wedges.

8 oz	goat cheese, cubed	250 g
3½ oz	cream cheese, cubed	100 g
1	clove garlic, halved	1
½ cup	dry white wine	125 mL
5 oz	smoked salmon, sliced into bite-size pieces	150 g
2	green onions, minced	2

1. In a bowl, combine goat cheese and cream cheese; mix well. Set aside.

2. Rub the inside of a large saucepan with cut sides of garlic. Discard garlic. Add wine; bring to a simmer over medium heat. Reduce heat to medium-low.

3. Add cheese mixture in small amounts to saucepan, stirring constantly after each addition with a wooden spoon in a figure-eight motion until cheese is melted.

4. Stir in smoked salmon; mix well. Transfer to fondue pot and garnish with green onions. Serve immediately.

Four-Cheese and Artichoke Fondue

1	jar (6 oz/170 mL) marinated artichoke hearts	1
6 oz	goat cheese, cubed	175 g
4 oz	Gruyère cheese, grated	125 g
3 oz	Asiago cheese, grated	90 g
1 oz	Parmesan cheese (preferably Parmigiano-Reggiano), freshly grated	30 g
1 tbsp	all-purpose flour	15 mL
½ cup	dry white wine	125 mL
1	clove garlic, minced	1

1. Drain artichokes, reserving 1 tbsp (15 mL) marinade.

2. In a bowl, combine goat cheese, Gruyère, Asiago, Parmesan and flour; mix well to coat cheese with flour. Set aside.

3. In a large saucepan, combine white wine and reserved 1 tbsp (15 mL) artichoke marinade; bring to a simmer over medium heat. Reduce heat to medium-low. Stir in minced garlic.

4. Add cheese mixture by handfuls to saucepan, whisking constantly after each addition in a figure-eight motion until cheese is melted.

5. Remove from heat and stir artichokes into melted cheese. Transfer to fondue pot and serve immediately.

Serves 4

Artichokes are native to the Mediterranean, and were brought to North America by French and Italian explorers. The tangy marinade gives this fondue a unique (although somewhat sour) flavor.

Tips
Asiago is a hard Italian cheese that melts easily and infuses this fondue with a robust flavor.

If you possibly can, use freshly grated Parmigiano-Reggiano. It's worth the expense! Prepackaged dry Parmesan is cheaper, but lacks both flavor and texture.

Make ahead
Cube goat cheese and grate Gruyère, Asiago and Parmesan. Combine in a bowl and refrigerate until needed.

Serve with...
Cubes of crusty Italian and sourdough bread, cubed panini rolls, and chunks of salami or pepperoni.

Goat Cheese and Thyme Fondue

Serves 4

Goat cheese, also known as chèvre, has a complex flavor that balances the cream cheese.

Make ahead

Cube goat cheese and cream cheese and combine in a bowl; refrigerate until needed.

Serve with...

Cubes of French bread or pumpernickel, breadsticks, pear and apple sections.

8 oz	goat cheese, cubed	250 g
4 oz	cream cheese, cubed	125 g
1 tbsp	all-purpose flour	15 mL
1	clove garlic, halved	1
¾ cup	dry white wine	175 mL
2 tbsp	chopped fresh thyme	25 mL
	Freshly ground black pepper to taste	

1. In a bowl, combine goat cheese, cream cheese and flour; mix well to coat cheese with flour. Set aside.

2. Rub the inside of a large saucepan with cut sides of garlic. Discard garlic. Add wine; bring to a simmer over medium heat. Reduce heat to medium-low.

3. Add cheese mixture in small amounts to saucepan, stirring constantly after each addition with a wooden spoon in a figure-eight motion until cheese is melted.

4. Stir in fresh thyme; mix well. Transfer to fondue pot and serve immediately.

Creamy Garlic, Onion and Herb Fondue

4 oz	Asiago cheese, grated	125 g
4 oz	cream cheese, softened, cubed	125 g
4 oz	goat cheese, cubed	125 g
1 tbsp	all-purpose flour	15 mL
¾ cup	dry white wine	175 mL
1 tbsp	freshly squeezed lime juice	15 mL
2 tbsp	minced Vidalia onion (or other sweet variety)	25 mL
2	cloves garlic, minced	2
1 tbsp	minced fresh basil	15 mL
1 tbsp	minced fresh chives	15 mL
1 tbsp	minced fresh lemon thyme	15 mL

1. In a bowl, combine Asiago, cream cheese, goat cheese and flour; mix well to coat cheese with flour. Set aside.

2. In a large saucepan, combine white wine, lime juice, onion and garlic; bring to a simmer over medium heat. Reduce heat to medium-low.

3. Add cheese mixture by handfuls to saucepan, whisking constantly after each addition in a figure-eight motion until cheese is melted.

4. Remove from heat. Stir in basil, chives and lemon thyme; mix well. Transfer to fondue pot and serve immediately.

Serves 4

Tips
Fresh herbs are a must for this fondue. If you don't have any lemon thyme or basil, substitute other fresh herbs that are available.

Chives are native to Asia and belong to the same family as garlic, onion, and leek. If you can't find fresh chives, use green onions (green part only) instead. Use kitchen shears to cut chives finely.

Make ahead
Grate Asiago and cube cream cheese and goat cheese. Combine in a bowl and refrigerate until needed.

Mince onion and garlic.

Wash and mince fresh herbs.

Serve with...
Blanched broccoli and cauliflower (see tip, page 61), fresh zucchini slices, fresh mushroom caps, focaccia, breadsticks.

Greek Feta and Mint Fondue

Serves 4

The unmistakable flavors of feta and goat cheese make a great combination in this recipe.

Tip

Mint is a perennial plant that, once established, can easily take over your garden. Similarly, the flavor of mint tends to overpower the taste of other ingredients — so don't add too much. For the best results, pick mint leaves just before flowering.

Make ahead

Crumble feta and cube goat cheese. Combine in a bowl and refrigerate until ready to use.

Wash and chop fresh dill and mint.

Serve with...

Pita triangles, croissant chunks, cherry tomatoes, steamed new potatoes, fresh spinach leaves (stacked in twos, folded then speared and dipped), cucumber slices.

4 oz	feta cheese, crumbled	125 g
2 oz	goat cheese, cubed	60 g
1 cup	milk	250 mL
1 tbsp	butter	15 mL
2 tbsp	all-purpose flour	25 mL
1 tsp	minced fresh dill	5 mL
1 tsp	chopped fresh mint	5 mL
¼ tsp	garlic powder	1 mL
Pinch	freshly ground black pepper	Pinch

1. In a bowl, combine feta and goat cheese. Set aside.

2. In a large saucepan over medium heat, stir together milk and butter. Heat until hot (but not boiling). Add flour a little bit at a time, whisking constantly until thickened. Reduce heat to low.

3. Add cheese mixture by handfuls to saucepan, whisking constantly after each addition in a figure-eight motion until cheese is melted.

4. Remove from heat. Stir in dill, mint, garlic powder and pepper; mix well. Transfer to fondue pot and serve immediately.

Camembert and Wild Mushroom Fondue

½ oz	mixed dried wild or exotic mushrooms, or porcini mushrooms	15 g
1 lb	Camembert cheese, trimmed of rind and cubed	500 g
1 tbsp	cornstarch	15 mL
1	clove garlic, halved	1
¾ cup	dry white wine	175 mL
1 tsp	dried rosemary	5 mL

Serves 6

Creamy Camembert was first produced in the village of Camembert, in the Normandy region of France. Triple-crème French Camembert offers the best results.

1. In a small bowl, soak mushrooms in 1 cup (250 mL) boiling water for 15 minutes. Drain mushrooms, chop and set aside.

2. In a bowl, combine Camembert and cornstarch; mix well to coat cheese with cornstarch. Set aside.

3. Rub the inside of a large saucepan with cut sides of garlic. Discard garlic. Add wine; bring to a simmer over medium heat. Reduce heat to medium-low.

4. Add cheese mixture by handfuls to saucepan, stirring constantly after each addition with a wooden spoon in a figure-eight motion until cheese is melted.

5. Stir in chopped wild mushrooms and rosemary; mix well. Transfer to fondue pot and serve immediately.

Tips
Once dried, wild mushrooms take on a more intense flavor and aroma.

You may substitute fresh wild mushrooms, sliced and sautéed in butter until softened, for the rehydrated dried mushrooms.

Make ahead
Trim and discard rind from Camembert; cut into cubes. Refrigerate until ready to use.

Serve with...
Cubes of crusty French bread, Italian bread or walnut bread, lightly toasted pita bread wedges.

Camembert and Pesto Fondue

This fondue pairs well with vegetables. Try lightly blanched broccoli and cauliflower florets, as well as asparagus.

Tips

Buy imported triple-crème French Camembert for best results.

Pine nuts are blanched seeds from pine cones, primarily from southern France, Italy and the southern United States. These pine trees only start producing seeds after 25 years and reach their commercial potential at 75 years old. In addition, seeds must typically be harvested by hand. No wonder pine nuts are so expensive!

Brown pine nuts in a nonstick skillet for about 2 minutes over medium heat, turning once.

Make ahead

Prepare the pesto (see Step 1) in advance.

Serve with...
Cubes of French bread, blanched vegetables, fresh mushrooms.

¼ cup	chopped fresh basil	50 mL
2	cloves garlic, minced	2
2 tsp	olive oil	10 mL
1 tbsp	pine nuts, toasted	15 mL
½ oz	Parmesan cheese (preferably Parmigiano-Reggiano), freshly grated	15 g
12 oz	Camembert cheese, trimmed and cubed	375 g
2 oz	Gruyère cheese, grated	60 g
1 tbsp	all-purpose flour	15 mL
½ cup	red wine	125 mL

1. In food processor or blender, combine basil, garlic, olive oil, pine nuts and Parmesan. Process until finely minced. Set aside.

2. In a bowl, combine Camembert, Gruyère and flour; mix well to coat cheese with flour. Set aside.

3. In a large saucepan, bring red wine to a simmer over medium heat. Reduce heat to medium-low.

4. Add cheese mixture by handfuls to saucepan, whisking constantly after each addition in a figure-eight motion until cheese is melted. (If fondue is too thin, whisk in additional flour, 1 tsp (5 mL) at a time, until desired consistency is reached.)

5. Remove saucepan from heat and whisk in reserved pesto mixture until well combined. Transfer to fondue pot and serve immediately.

Brie and Sun-Dried Tomato Fondue

3 tbsp	dry-packed sun-dried tomatoes	45 mL
8 oz	Brie cheese, trimmed of rind and cubed	250 g
1 tbsp	cornstarch	15 mL
1 tbsp	butter	15 mL
1	shallot, minced	1
½ cup	dry white wine	125 mL
1 tbsp	granulated sugar	15 mL

1. Soak sun-dried tomatoes in boiling water to cover for 20 minutes. Drain, pat dry and chop (or cut with scissors) into small pieces. Set aside.

2. In a bowl, toss cubed Brie with cornstarch until well coated. Set aside.

3. In a large saucepan, melt butter over medium heat. Add shallots and sauté until softened. Add white wine and heat just until simmering. Reduce heat to medium-low.

4. Add Brie mixture by handfuls to saucepan, stirring constantly after each addition with a wooden spoon in a figure-eight motion until the cheese is melted.

5. Stir in sun-dried tomatoes and sugar; mix well. Transfer to fondue pot and serve immediately.

Serves 4

Tips
Be sure to trim rind from Brie; it does not melt well and adds an unpleasantly strong flavor.

Imported French (not domestic) Brie is best for this recipe.

Prechopped sun-dried tomatoes are available in some bulk food or health stores. These save preparation time, and are oil-free.

Use kitchen shears to cut up rehydrated sun-dried tomatoes.

Make ahead
Trim and discard rind from Brie; cut into cubes. Refrigerate until ready to use.

Serve with...
Focaccia in wedges, cubes of croissants or French rolls.

Brie Fondue with Caramelized Onions

Serves 4

Caramelized onions marry beautifully with Brie.

Tips
Use Vidalia onions from Vidalia, Georgia, if possible. They produce the most delectable caramelized onions because of their delicate sweetness.

Imported French Brie is best for this recipe.

Make ahead
Trim and discard rind from Brie; cut into cubes. Refrigerate until ready to use.

Serve with...
Focaccia wedges, cubes of French or sourdough bread, marinated mushrooms, pickled onions.

1 tbsp	olive oil	15 mL
1	large onion, sliced	1
1 tbsp	granulated sugar	15 mL
1 tbsp	balsamic vinegar	15 mL
1 tsp	Worcestershire sauce	5 mL
12 oz	Brie cheese, trimmed of rind and cubed	375 g
1 tbsp	cornstarch	15 mL
1	clove garlic, halved	1
¾ cup	dry white wine	175 mL

1. In a nonstick skillet, heat olive oil over low heat. Sauté onion until translucent, about 8 minutes. Sprinkle with sugar, cover and cook for 8 minutes. Sprinkle with vinegar and Worcestershire sauce; cook, uncovered, stirring frequently, for about 2 minutes or until onion is caramelized.

2. In a bowl, combine Brie and cornstarch; mix well to coat cheese with cornstarch. Set aside.

3. Rub the inside of a large saucepan with cut sides of garlic. Add wine; bring to a simmer over medium heat. Reduce heat to medium-low.

4. Add cheese mixture by handfuls to saucepan, stirring constantly after each addition with a wooden spoon in a figure-eight motion until cheese is melted.

5. Stir in caramelized onion; mix well. Transfer to fondue pot and serve immediately.

Sweet Brie Fondue

8 oz	Brie cheese, trimmed of rind and cubed	250 g
1 tbsp	all-purpose flour	15 mL
¾ cup	dry white wine, divided	175 mL
3 tbsp	packed brown sugar	45 mL
1 tsp	ground cinnamon	5 mL
2 tbsp	brandy	25 mL

1. In a large bowl, toss Brie cubes with flour until well coated. Set aside.

2. In a large saucepan, bring ½ cup (125 mL) of the wine to a simmer over medium heat. Reduce heat to medium-low.

3. Add one-quarter of Brie cubes to saucepan, whisking constantly in a figure-eight motion until cheese is melted. Repeat procedure with second and third quarter of Brie cubes. Whisk in brown sugar and cinnamon. Add remaining Brie cubes and whisk until melted through.

4. Stir brandy into mixture. If too thick, add enough of remaining white wine to achieve desired consistency. Transfer to fondue pot and serve immediately.

Serves 4

This is great as a dessert fondue or as a sweet starter. Serve it with a chilled dry white wine.

Make ahead

Trim and cube Brie. Refrigerate until needed.

Serve with...

Plain French or sourdough bread (as an appetizer); angel food cake or pound cake cubes, apple wedges, ladyfingers and orange sections (as a dessert).

Oil fondues

Oil fondues

Ingredients

OIL FONDUES ARE THE MOST straightforward type to prepare. Their simplicity is exemplified by the Classic Beef Bourguignonne (see recipe, page 78), which involves frying strips or cubes of beef tenderloin in oil and then dipping the cooked meat in a range of sauces.

As a rule, I recommend using tender cuts of meat, such as beef tenderloin, pork tenderloin or loin of lamb. Lesser-quality meats will save you money, but will produce tough results.

Which oil you use for fondue is a matter of personal preference. Peanut oil is recommended because it has a higher smoking point than other oils, but it is very expensive. Vegetable oil works equally well, and you may want to experiment with shortening to determine your inclination. Vegetable oils can include olive, canola, safflower or corn oil.

In the fondue pot

OIL FONDUES REQUIRE a pot capable of withstanding more heat than is required by other types of fondue. For this reason, do not use a ceramic or earthenware fondue pot. Instead, use fondue pots made of enameled cast iron or other metals, such as stainless steel or copper.

You can use a traditional set-up, with the pot set over an alcohol burner, but electric fondues are the most convenient, since oil can be heated directly in the pot and the temperature is easily controlled with a thermostat. Conventional pots require that the oil be preheated in a saucepan on the stove to 375°F (190°C) — or just below boiling. To test the temperature, drop a cube of bread into the oil; it should turn golden brown in about 30 seconds.

Set the fondue pot on the fondue stand and place splatter shield on pot. Carefully pour heated oil into the fondue pot to no more than half full. Fill the alcohol burner as directed and light the burner with a match. Adjust flame to desired level with movable handle.

Serving the fondue

PROVIDE EACH GUEST with several fondue forks, regular cutlery and a paper towel–lined bowl for patting off excess oil, as well as an assortment of dips and sauces.

Any food, as well as the metal fondue fork holding it, becomes extremely hot after being immersed in hot oil. Guests should pat the morsel off on a paper towel to eliminate excess oil, remove the fried food from the fondue fork, and then eat it with a regular fork.

Limit six fondue forks to the oil fondue at one time — or the temperature of the oil will drop too low. Advise guests to remove their fondue fork from the hot oil and, while the meat is cooling, spear the next piece of meat and place in fondue pot.

Plan on 4 to 6 oz (125 to 175 g) per person for a main-course meat or seafood fondue with other side dishes. Heartier appetites will require 6 to 8 oz (175 to 250 g).

Sauces play an important role in oil fondues. You can make your own dips ahead of time or take advantage of the many prepared dips and sauces now available in your supermarket. Sauces should be served warm or at room temperature; four choices is optimal.

Centrally locate the main platter of raw meat, poultry or seafood on the table, allowing guests easy access. Meat or poultry should be cubed or sliced thinly into strips and brought to room temperature before fonduing. If the meat has been marinated, pat it off slightly with a paper towel to avoid oil splatters. Dry rubs provide great flavor and stick to the meat. Meat or other foods should be cooked for 1 to 2 minutes in oil fondue or until cooked to desired doneness.

Each guest skewers a piece of meat, poultry or seafood, which is dunked in the oil fondue pot for cooking. It generally takes 1 to 2 minutes to cook meat in oil, but each person can decide how long to fondue according to personal preference.

Classic Beef Bourguignonne

Beef Bourguignonne, the original oil fondue, must be served with a selection of dipping sauces. These can be store-bought or homemade, and should provide a balance of different flavors, such as sweet, spicy, tangy and creamy.

Tip
Use only premium, high-quality beef (such as beef tenderloin) for this recipe. Remove all fat before using.

Make ahead
Cut beef tenderloin into 1-inch (2.5 cm) cubes. Place on platter and refrigerate until needed.

Whip up some homemade sauces.

Serve with...
Sweet-and-sour sauce, Thai peanut sauce, wasabi mayonnaise, aïoli.

	Oil for fondue	
1 lb	beef tenderloin, at room temperature, trimmed and cut into 1-inch (2.5 cm) cubes	500 g

1. In a saucepan, heat oil to 375°F (190°C) and transfer to fondue pot (or heat oil in an electric fondue). Do not fill fondue pot more than half full.

2. Spear cube of beef with fondue fork and fondue for 1 to 2 minutes. Once cooked, transfer beef to a paper towel–lined plate (each person should have their own) and pat off any excess oil. Dip cubes in sauce(s) as desired.

Beef with Sweet-and-Sour Marinade

Marinade

3 tbsp	vegetable oil	45 mL
3 tbsp	red wine	45 mL
2 tbsp	vinegar	25 mL
2 tbsp	water	25 mL
1 tbsp	packed brown sugar	15 mL
1 tbsp	ketchup	15 mL
1	clove garlic, minced	1
1 tbsp	minced gingerroot	15 mL
½ tsp	garam masala	2 mL
	Salt and freshly ground black pepper to taste	
1 lb	beef tenderloin, thinly sliced and cut into 1-inch (2.5 cm) strips	500 g
	Oil for fondue	

1. *Marinade:* In a bowl, whisk together oil, wine, vinegar, water, brown sugar, ketchup, garlic, ginger, garam marsala and salt and pepper to taste.

2. Place beef in a shallow casserole; pour marinade over and toss to coat. Cover and marinate for at least 1 hour in refrigerator.

3. In a saucepan, heat oil to 375°F (190°C) and transfer to fondue pot (or heat oil in an electric fondue). Do not fill fondue pot more than half full.

4. Remove each beef slice from marinade, shaking off any excess. Pat dry with a paper towel. Roll up slice and spear with fondue fork. Fondue for 1 to 2 minutes or until cooked to desired doneness.

Serves 4

Tips
If you don't have an electric fondue pot, you will need to use a cooking thermometer to check the temperature of the oil as it heats in the saucepan. Watch it carefully and never leave hot oil unattended.

Before immersing it in hot oil, pat beef with a paper towel to absorb excess marinade; this will help to prevent spattering.

Make ahead
Complete to the end of Step 2. Refrigerate until needed.

Serve with...
Asian dipping sauce, sweet mustard dip, Thai peanut sauce, fried rice, steamed vegetables.

Caribbean Beef Fondue

Awaken your taste buds with the exciting essence of the Caribbean.

Tip
You can substitute pork or chicken for the beef.

Make ahead
Complete to the end of Step 4. Refrigerate until needed.

Serve with...
Horseradish dip, honey mustard, mango chutney.

½ cup	all-purpose flour	125 mL
1 tsp	dried thyme	5 mL
½ tsp	hot pepper flakes	2 mL
¼ tsp	garlic powder	1 mL
	Salt and freshly ground black pepper to taste	
2	eggs	2
1 cup	corn flakes cereal crumbs	250 mL
2 tsp	ground cumin	10 mL
1 tsp	ground coriander	5 mL
½ tsp	ground ginger	2 mL
¼ tsp	ground allspice	1 mL
1 lb	beef sirloin or flank steak, thinly sliced and cut into 1-inch (2.5 cm) strips	500 g
	Oil for fondue	

1. In a bowl, combine flour with thyme, hot pepper flakes, garlic powder, salt and black pepper.

2. In a second bowl, beat eggs.

3. In a third bowl, combine corn flakes crumbs with cumin, coriander, ginger and allspice.

4. Dip beef pieces one at a time in flour mixture, then egg, then corn flakes crumbs. Set beef strips on a platter.

5. In a saucepan, heat oil to 375°F (190°C) and transfer to fondue pot (or heat oil in an electric fondue). Do not fill fondue pot more than half full.

6. Spear beef with fondue fork and fondue for 1 to 2 minutes or until golden brown.

Ginger Beef Fondue

Marinade

¼ cup	cider vinegar	50 mL
¼ cup	water	50 mL
2 tbsp	chili sauce	25 mL
2 tbsp	finely minced crystallized ginger	25 mL
1 tbsp	light (fancy) molasses	15 mL
1 tsp	curry powder	5 mL
1 lb	beef tenderloin, thinly sliced and cut into 1-inch (2.5 cm) strips	500 g
	Oil for fondue	

1. *Marinade:* In a bowl, whisk together cider vinegar, water, chili sauce, crystallized ginger, molasses and curry powder until well blended.

2. In a shallow casserole, cover beef strips with marinade, tossing to coat well. Cover and refrigerate for at least 1 hour.

3. Remove beef strips from marinade, shaking off any excess. Pat dry with a paper towel. Roll up strips and and set aside on a platter decorated with parsley and crystallized ginger.

4. In a saucepan, heat oil to 375°F (190°C) and transfer to fondue pot (or heat oil in an electric fondue). Do not fill fondue pot more than half full.

5. Spear rolled ginger beef with fondue fork and fondue for 1 to 2 minutes or until cooked to desired doneness.

Serves 4

The crystallized ginger in this recipe adds a spectacular flavor and aroma.

Tip
Remember to shake off excess marinade to avoid spattering.

Make ahead
Complete to the end of Step 2. Refrigerate until needed.

Serve with...
Asian dipping sauce, plain soy sauce, mango salsa or chutney, Basmati rice, stir-fried vegetables.

Korean Fondue

Marinade

2 tbsp	soy sauce	25 mL
2 tbsp	water	25 mL
1 tbsp	minced green onions	15 mL
2	cloves garlic, minced	2
1 tsp	granulated sugar	5 mL
½ tsp	ground ginger	2 mL
	Freshly ground black pepper to taste	
1 lb	flank steak or boneless skinless chicken breasts, thinly sliced and cut into 1-inch (2.5 cm) strips	500 g
2 tsp	sesame seeds, toasted	10 mL
	Oil for fondue	

1. *Marinade:* In a bowl, combine soy sauce, water, green onions, garlic, sugar, ginger and pepper; stir well to combine.

2. In a shallow casserole, cover steak or chicken strips with marinade, tossing to coat well. Roll each strip in sesame seeds. Cover and refrigerate at least 2 hours for steak or 1 hour for chicken.

3. In a saucepan, heat oil to 375°F (190°C) and transfer to fondue pot (or heat oil in an electric fondue). Do not fill fondue pot more than half full.

4. Spear steak or chicken with fondue fork and fondue for 1 to 2 minutes or until cooked to desired doneness.

Maple Beef Fondue

Marinade

½ cup	pure maple syrup (the real stuff, not "maple-flavored"!)	125 mL
1 tbsp	chili sauce	15 mL
1 tbsp	Worcestershire sauce	15 mL
1 tbsp	red wine vinegar	15 mL
1 tbsp	dried onion flakes	15 mL
½ tsp	dry mustard	2 mL
	Salt and freshly ground black pepper to taste	
1 lb	beef tenderloin, thinly sliced and cut into 1-inch (2.5 cm) strips	500 g
	Oil for fondue	

1. *Marinade:* In a small saucepan over medium-low heat, combine maple syrup, chili sauce, Worcestershire, vinegar, onion flakes, mustard, salt and pepper. Bring to a boil and cook, stirring occasionally, for 2 minutes or until thickened. Remove from heat and set aside to cool to lukewarm.

2. In a shallow casserole, pour marinade over beef, tossing to coat well. Cover and refrigerate for at least 1 hour.

3. In a saucepan, heat oil to 375°F (190°C) and transfer to fondue pot (or heat oil in an electric fondue). Do not fill fondue pot more than half full.

4. Spear beef with fondue fork and fondue for 1 to 2 minutes or until cooked to desired doneness.

Serves 4

For a "maple-themed" meal, serve this with Maple Cheese Fondue (see recipe, page 34) as an appetizer.

Tip
This recipe makes enough marinade to coat the meat, but not enough to drench it! If the marinade is too wet, you'll need to shake off the excess and pat the meat dry.

Make ahead
Complete to the end of Step 2. Refrigerate until needed.

Serve with...
Mustard, zesty mayonnaise, Thai peanut sauce.

Smoky Beef Nuggets

Serves 4

Tips
In place of cracker crumbs, use panko crumbs or dried bread crumbs.

For a different flavor, use boneless skinless turkey or chicken breast.

Make ahead
Complete to the end of Step 3. Refrigerate. Bring to room temperature for 20 minutes before fonduing in oil.

Serve with...
Honey dill dip, honey mustard, blue cheese dip, red pepper aïoli.

½ cup	all-purpose flour	125 mL
½ cup	cracker crumbs (such as soda crackers or stoned wheat crackers)	125 mL
¼ cup	freshly grated Parmesan cheese (optional)	50 mL
1 tbsp	smoked paprika	15 mL
1 tbsp	dried onion flakes	15 mL
1 tsp	cayenne pepper	5 mL
1 tsp	garlic powder	5 mL
	Salt and freshly ground black pepper to taste	
2	eggs	2
1 lb	beef flank or top sirloin steak, cut into 1-inch (2.5 cm) cubes	500 g
	Oil for fondue	

1. In a bowl, combine flour, cracker crumbs, Parmesan (if using), paprika, onion flakes, cayenne, garlic powder, salt and black pepper.

2. In a second bowl, beat eggs.

3. Dip beef pieces one at a time in egg, then flour mixture. Set beef nuggets on a platter.

4. In a saucepan, heat oil to 375°F (190°C) and transfer to fondue pot (or heat oil in an electric fondue). Do not fill fondue pot more than half full.

5. Spear beef nuggets with fondue fork and fondue for 1 to 2 minutes or until golden brown.

Teriyaki Beef or Chicken Fondue

Marinade

1/3 cup	soy sauce	75 mL
1/4 cup	liquid honey	50 mL
2 tbsp	vegetable oil	25 mL
2	cloves garlic, minced	2
1 1/2 tsp	grated gingerroot	7 mL
1 tsp	finely minced onion	5 mL
1 lb	beef tenderloin or boneless skinless chicken breast, thinly sliced and cut into 1-inch (2.5 cm) strips	500 g
	Oil for fondue	

1. *Marinade:* In a bowl, combine soy sauce, honey, oil, garlic, ginger and onion; mix well.

2. In a shallow casserole, pour marinade over beef (or chicken), tossing to coat well. Cover and refrigerate for at least 1 hour.

3. In a saucepan, heat oil to 375°F (190°C) and transfer to fondue pot (or heat oil in an electric fondue). Do not fill fondue pot more than half full.

4. Remove beef or chicken from marinade, shaking off any excess, and pat dry with a paper towel. Spear one piece with fondue fork and fondue for about 2 minutes.

Serves 4

Tip
If honey is too solid to combine in marinade, melt first in microwave on Low for 15 seconds.

Make ahead
Complete to the end of Step 2. Refrigerate until needed.

Serve with...
Thai peanut sauce, sticky rice and stir-fried vegetables

Chinese Breaded Veal Fondue

Tips

Chinese five-spice powder is typically a mixture of anise, cinnamon, cloves, Szechwan pepper and ground ginger. Its distinguishing feature is the licorice flavor that comes from star anise or licorice root.

For less ginger flavor, omit the added ground ginger.

Make ahead

Complete to the end of Step 4. Refrigerate. Bring to room temperature for 20 minutes before fonduing in oil.

Serve with...

Plum sauce, Thai peanut sauce, sweet-and-sour sauce.

1 cup	all-purpose flour	250 mL
½ tsp	Chinese five-spice powder	2 mL
¼ tsp	garlic powder	1 mL
¼ tsp	salt	1 mL
Pinch	freshly ground black pepper	Pinch
2	eggs	2
1 lb	veal shoulder, cut into 1-inch (2.5 cm) cubes	500 g
½ cup	dry bread crumbs	125 mL
¼ tsp	ground ginger	1 mL
	Oil for fondue	

1. In a bowl, combine flour, five-spice powder, garlic powder, salt and pepper.

2. In a second bowl, beat eggs.

3. In a third bowl, combine bread crumbs and ginger.

4. Dip veal slices one at a time in flour mixture, then egg, then bread crumbs. Set breaded veal on a platter.

5. In a saucepan, heat oil to 375°F (190°C) and transfer to fondue pot (or heat oil in an electric fondue). Do not fill fondue pot more than half full.

6. Spear breaded veal with fondue fork and fondue for 1 to 2 minutes or until golden brown.

Stuffed Veal Rolls

2 cups	dry bread crumbs	500 mL
1½ tsp	dried oregano	7 mL
1 tsp	dried tarragon	5 mL
1 tsp	garlic powder	5 mL
	Salt and freshly ground black pepper to taste	
2	eggs	2
1 oz	Gruyère cheese, cut into ½-inch (1 cm) cubes	30 g
1 lb	veal, thinly sliced and cut into 2-inch (5 cm) strips	500 g
	Oil for fondue	

1. In a bowl, combine bread crumbs, oregano, tarragon, garlic powder, salt and pepper. Mix well.

2. In another bowl, beat eggs.

3. Place a cube of cheese on 1 veal slice. Fold one side, then the other side of veal slice over cheese, sealing as well as possible. Dip in eggs, then coat thoroughly in bread crumb mixture. Repeat procedure until all rolls are filled and coated.

4. In a saucepan, heat oil to 375°F (190°C) and transfer to fondue pot (or heat oil in an electric fondue). Do not fill fondue pot more than half full.

5. Spear veal bundle on fondue fork and fondue for 2 to 3 minutes or until golden and veal is cooked through.

Serves 4

Tip
Leg of veal is usually sold cut in scallops. It is nice and tender, making it a good choice for this recipe.

Make ahead
Complete to the end of Step 3. Refrigerate. Bring to room temperature for 20 minutes before fonduing in oil.

Serve with...
Serve with plum sauce, barbecue sauce, garlic aïoli.

Veal Wiener Schnitzel Nuggets

Wiener schnitzel is typically light on spices, allowing the tender veal flavor to shine through.

Tip
You can use beef tenderloin in place of veal.

Make ahead
Complete to the end of Step 4. Refrigerate. Bring to room temperature for 20 minutes before fonduing in oil.

Serve with...
Fresh lemon wedges, sweet-and-sour sauce, tonkatsu sauce.

½ cup	all-purpose flour	125 mL
½ tsp	garlic powder	2 mL
½ tsp	salt	2 mL
¼ tsp	freshly ground black pepper	1 mL
2	eggs	2
1 cup	dry bread crumbs	250 mL
1 lb	veal scaloppine, cut into 1-inch (2.5 cm) strips	500 g
	Oil for fondue	

1. In a bowl, combine flour, garlic powder, salt and pepper.

2. In a second bowl, beat eggs.

3. In a third bowl, place bread crumbs.

4. Dip veal pieces one at a time in flour mixture, then egg, then bread crumbs. Set veal nuggets on a platter.

5. In a saucepan, heat oil to 375°F (190°C) and transfer to fondue pot (or heat oil in an electric fondue). Do not fill fondue pot more than half full.

6. Spear veal nuggets with fondue fork and fondue for 1 to 2 minutes or until golden brown.

Italian Meatball Fondue

8 oz	ground veal	250 g
8 oz	lean ground beef	250 g
1/3 cup	dry bread crumbs	75 mL
1	egg, beaten	1
1	clove garlic, minced	1
1 tbsp	chopped fresh basil (or 1 tsp/ 5 mL dried)	15 mL
1 tbsp	chopped fresh parsley (or 1 tsp/ 5 mL dried)	15 mL
1 tsp	dried Italian seasoning	5 mL
1 tsp	dried onion flakes	5 mL
	Salt and freshly ground black pepper to taste	
	Oil for fondue	

1. In a large bowl, combine veal, beef, bread crumbs, egg, garlic, basil, parsley, Italian seasoning, onion flakes, salt and pepper. Mix well. Using your hands, form into 40 meatballs, each about 1 inch (2.5 cm) in diameter.

2. Place on a baking sheet or platter lined with waxed paper and serve immediately or refrigerate until just before required. If refrigerated, place on counter for 15 minutes and bring to room temperature before fonduing.

3. In a saucepan, heat oil to 375°F (190°C) and transfer to fondue pot (or heat oil in an electric fondue). Do not fill fondue pot more than half full.

4. Spear meatball with fondue fork and fondue for 4 minutes or until cooked through and no longer pink inside

Serves 4

Fresh basil, readily available from spring through fall, enhances these meatballs.

Tip
For an Italian-themed menu, serve with an Italian cheese fondue.

Make ahead
Complete to the end of Step 2.

Serve with...
Gremolata, honey mustard, red pepper aïoli.

Mexican Meatball Fondue

Tips

Adjust the heat of these meatballs by adding more cayenne pepper or omitting it.

Like battered fondues, meatballs should be brought to room temperature before fonduing.

Make ahead

Complete to the end of Step 2.

Serve with...

Guacamole, sour cream, blue cheese dip, salsa verde.

1 lb	lean ground beef	500 g
1 cup	dry bread crumbs	250 mL
⅓ cup	chili sauce	75 mL
1	egg, beaten	1
1	clove garlic, minced	1
2 tbsp	finely minced cilantro	25 mL
1 tsp	dried onion flakes	5 mL
Pinch	cayenne pepper	Pinch
	Salt and freshly ground black pepper to taste	
	Oil for fondue	

1. In a large bowl, combine beef, bread crumbs, chili sauce, egg, garlic, cilantro, onion flakes, cayenne, salt and black pepper. Mix well. Using your hands, form into 40 meatballs, each about 1 inch (2.5 cm) in diameter.

2. Place on a baking sheet or platter lined with waxed paper and serve immediately or refrigerate until just before required. If refrigerated, place on counter for 15 minutes and bring to room temperature before fonduing.

3. In a saucepan, heat oil to 375°F (190°C) and transfer to fondue pot (or heat oil in an electric fondue). Do not fill fondue pot more than half full.

4. Spear meatball with fondue fork and fondue for 4 minutes or until cooked through and no longer pink inside.

Moroccan Meatball Fondue

1 lb	ground lamb	500 g
½ cup	instant couscous, cooked	125 mL
1	egg, beaten	1
1	clove garlic, minced	1
2 tbsp	finely minced onion	25 mL
1 tbsp	chopped fresh parsley	15 mL
½ tsp	dried coriander	2 mL
¼ tsp	ground cumin	1 mL
¼ tsp	ground ginger	1 mL
Pinch	ground cinnamon	Pinch
Pinch	ground allspice	Pinch
Pinch	cayenne pepper	Pinch
	Salt and freshly ground black pepper to taste	
	Oil for fondue	

Serves 4

If you are looking to lower your sodium intake, this fondue is for you. The meatballs are packed with herbs and spices, so you can use salt sparingly.

Tip
You can use ground beef instead of the lamb, although it won't be as authentic.

Make ahead
Cook couscous in advance.

Complete to the end of Step 2.

Serve with...
Tomato curry sauce, hummus, cilantro coulis, roasted red pepper dip.

1. In a large bowl, combine lamb, couscous, egg, garlic, onion, parsley, coriander, cumin, ginger, cinnamon, allspice, cayenne, salt and black pepper. Mix well. Using your hands, form into 40 meatballs, each about 1 inch (2.5 cm) in diameter.

2. Place on a baking sheet or platter lined with waxed paper and serve immediately or refrigerate until just before required. If refrigerated, place on counter for 15 minutes and bring to room temperature before fonduing.

3. In a saucepan, heat oil to 375°F (190°C) and transfer to fondue pot (or heat oil in an electric fondue). Do not fill fondue pot more than half full.

4. Spear meatball with fondue fork and fondue for 4 minutes or until cooked through and no longer pink inside.

Sausage Fondue with Tomato Sauce

Tips

Feel free to replace hot sausage with a milder variety if desired.

Instead of a fondue pot, use a chafing dish to keep tomato sauce warm.

If you can't find fresh herbs, use 1 tsp (5 mL) each dried oregano and dried basil.

Make ahead

Prepare tomato sauce early in the day. Reheat over low heat.

Serve with...

Freshly grated Parmesan cheese (sprinkled on sausage dipped in tomato sauce), pasta and salad.

Tomato Sauce

2 tsp	olive oil	10 mL
1	onion, chopped	1
2	cloves garlic, minced	2
1	can (19 oz/540 mL) crushed tomatoes	1
1½ tsp	granulated sugar	7 mL
1 tbsp	chopped fresh oregano	15 mL
1 tbsp	chopped fresh basil	15 mL
¼ tsp	hot pepper flakes	1 mL
	Salt and freshly ground black pepper to taste	
	Oil for fondue	
1 lb	hot Italian sausage, skins intact, cut into 1-inch (2.5 cm) chunks	500 g

1. *Tomato sauce:* In a large saucepan, heat oil over medium heat. Add onions and sauté for 3 minutes. Add garlic and sauté for another 2 minutes or until onions are translucent. Add crushed tomatoes and cook, stirring occasionally, until sauce comes to a boil. Reduce heat to low. Add sugar, oregano, basil, hot pepper flakes, salt and black pepper; simmer, uncovered (or with spatter screen), for about 20 minutes, allowing flavors to blend.

2. Transfer tomato sauce to earthenware or stainless steel fondue pot. Adjust alcohol burner flame to low.

3. In a saucepan, heat oil to 375°F (190°C) and transfer to fondue pot (or heat oil in an electric fondue). Do not fill fondue pot more than half full.

4. Spear sausage chunks (through skin sides) with fondue fork and fondue about 2 minutes. Dip in warm tomato sauce.

Sausage Meatballs Fondue

8 oz	Italian sausage, casings removed, meat crumbled	250 g
½	onion, minced	½
1	clove garlic, minced	1
2 oz	pickles, finely minced (about 2 medium)	60 g
¼ cup	cream cheese, softened	50 mL
1 tbsp	Dijon mustard	15 mL
½ tsp	paprika	2 mL
Pinch	freshly ground black pepper	Pinch
¼ cup	all-purpose flour	50 mL
2	eggs	2
1 cup	bread crumbs	250 mL
	Oil for fondue	

1. In skillet over medium heat, brown sausage, onion and garlic until sausage is cooked through. Drain fat from skillet. Stir in minced pickles and set aside.

2. In a bowl, combine cream cheese, mustard, paprika and pepper. Blend until smooth. Add to sausage mixture, combining well. Refrigerate for 15 minutes.

3. Place flour on a plate. In a small bowl, beat eggs. Put bread crumbs on another plate or in a shallow bowl.

4. Using your hands, form sausage mixture into balls. Coat meatball with flour, then dip in beaten eggs, then roll in bread crumbs. Repeat until all meatballs are coated. Refrigerate until needed, bringing to room temperature for 15 minutes before serving.

5. In a saucepan, heat oil to 375°F (190°C) and transfer to fondue pot (or heat oil in an electric fondue). Do not fill fondue pot more than half full.

6. Spear meatball with fondue fork and fondue for 2 minutes or until golden brown.

Serves 4

Tips
To hold meatballs securely, it's best to use a wide fondue fork, since its tines are further apart than those of a conventional fondue fork.

Try this recipe with ground turkey in place of sausage.

Make ahead
Complete to the end of Step 4. Refrigerate. Bring to room temperature for 20 minutes before fonduing in oil.

Serve with...
Sweet-and-sour sauce, mustard mayonnaise dip, tomato curry sauce.

Cajun Pork

Serves 4

Tips

In place of bread crumbs, finely process or crush soda crackers in a blender.

For a different flavor, use boneless skinless turkey or chicken breast.

Make ahead

Complete to the end of Step 4. Refrigerate. Bring to room temperature for 20 minutes before fonduing in oil.

Serve with...

Honey dill dip, blue cheese dip, honey mustard.

¼ cup	all-purpose flour	50 mL
¼ tsp	onion powder	1 mL
¼ tsp	garlic powder	1 mL
	Salt and freshly ground black pepper to taste	
2	eggs	2
1 cup	dry bread crumbs	250 mL
1 tbsp	Cajun seasoning	15 mL
1 tbsp	dried onion flakes	15 mL
1 lb	pork tenderloin, cut into 1-inch (2.5 cm) cubes	500 g
	Oil for fondue	

1. In a large bowl, combine flour, onion powder, garlic powder, salt and pepper.

2. In a second bowl, beat eggs.

3. In a third bowl, combine bread crumbs with Cajun seasoning and dried onion flakes.

4. Dip pork cubes one at a time in flour mixture, then egg, then bread crumbs. Set breaded pork on a platter.

5. In a saucepan, heat oil to 375°F (190°C) and transfer to fondue pot (or heat oil in an electric fondue). Do not fill fondue pot more than half full.

6. Spear breaded pork with fondue fork and fondue for 1 to 2 minutes or until golden brown.

Cumin Pork

Marinade

1½ tbsp	whole cumin seeds	22 mL
1 tbsp	ground coriander	15 mL
2	cloves garlic, minced	2
1½ tbsp	olive oil	22 mL
2 tsp	chili sauce	10 mL
1 lb	pork tenderloin, cut into 1-inch (2.5 cm) cubes	500 g
	Salt and freshly ground black pepper to taste	
	Oil for fondue	

1. *Marinade:* In a bowl, combine cumin, coriander, garlic, olive oil and chili sauce; mix well to make a smooth paste.

2. Season pork cubes with salt and pepper. Rub cubes with paste; cover and refrigerate for at least 1 hour.

3. In a saucepan, heat oil to 375°F (190°C) and transfer to fondue pot (or heat oil in an electric fondue). Do not fill fondue pot more than half full.

4. Spear pork cube with fondue fork and fondue for 1 to 2 minutes or until cooked to desired doneness.

Serves 4

Tips

Garnish serving platter of pork cubes with fresh coriander.

You can substitute beef if you wish, but cumin and pork are a superior combination.

This is more a rub than a wet marinade, so you don't need to pat off the pork before immersing in oil.

Make ahead

Complete to the end of Step 2. Refrigerate until needed.

Serve with...

Thai peanut sauce, plum sauce, aïoli.

Hawaiian Pork

Serves 4

Tips
Try this recipe using chicken instead of pork.

Sprinkle 2 tbsp (25 mL) coconut in reserved marinade to add texture to dipping sauce.

Make ahead
Complete to the end of Step 2. Refrigerate until needed.

Serve with...
Reserved marinade as dipping sauce, mango salsa or chutney, Thai peanut sauce, garlic aïoli.

Marinade

1	can (19 oz/540 mL) crushed pineapple, with juice	1
½ cup	finely minced onion	125 mL
½ cup	liquid honey	125 mL
¼ cup	vinegar	50 mL
1 tbsp	soy sauce	15 mL
3	cloves garlic, minced	3
1 tbsp	finely minced gingerroot	15 mL
1 tsp	ground coriander	5 mL
1 tsp	cornstarch	5 mL
	Salt and freshly ground black pepper to taste	
1 lb	pork tenderloin, cut into 1-inch (2.5 cm) cubes	500 g
	Oil for fondue	

1. *Marinade:* In a saucepan over medium-low heat, combine pineapple, onion, honey, vinegar, soy sauce, garlic, ginger, coriander, cornstarch, salt and pepper. Stir until honey is melted and ingredients are blended. Remove from heat and set aside to cool to room temperature.

2. In a shallow casserole, pour 2¼ cups (300 mL) of the marinade over pork tenderloin, tossing to coat well. Cover and refrigerate for at least 1 hour. (The remaining ¾ cup/175 mL marinade will be used for dipping.)

3. In a saucepan, heat oil to 375°F (190°C) and transfer to fondue pot (or heat oil in an electric fondue). Do not fill fondue pot more than half full.

4. Remove pork cube from marinade, shaking off any excess. Pat dry with a paper towel. Spear pork with fondue fork and fondue 1 to 2 minutes or until cooked to desired doneness.

Queso Fondido (page 54)

Pizza Fondue (page 57)

Roasted Red Pepper and
Mozzarella Fondue (page 58)

Smoked Salmon and Cream Cheese Fondue (page 64)

Camembert and Wild Mushroom Fondue (page 69)

Caribbean Beef Fondue (page 80) with Honey Mustard (page 251)

Mexican Meatball Fondue (page 90) with
Blue Cheese Dip (page 242) and Salsa Verde (page 247)

Sausage Fondue with Tomato Sauce (page 92)

Maple-Glazed Pork Medallions

Marinade

¼ cup	pure maple syrup	50 mL
1 tbsp	vegetable oil	25 mL
1 tbsp	Dijon mustard	15 mL
3	cloves garlic, minced	3
¼ tsp	freshly ground black pepper	1 mL
1 lb	pork tenderloin, thinly sliced and cut into 1-inch (2.5 cm) strips	500 g
	Oil for fondue	

1. *Marinade:* In a bowl, combine maple syrup, oil, mustard, garlic and pepper; mix well.

2. In a shallow casserole, pour marinade over pork, tossing to coat well. Cover and refrigerate for at least 1 hour.

3. Remove pork strips from marinade, shaking off any excess. Pat dry with a paper towel. Roll up strips and set aside on a platter.

4. In a saucepan, heat oil to 375°F (190°C) and transfer to fondue pot (or heat oil in an electric fondue). Do not fill fondue pot more than half full.

5. Spear rolled pork with fondue fork and fondue for 1 to 2 minutes or until cooked to desired doneness.

Serves 4

Maple-glazed pork medallions are a sweet and savory main dish fondue.

Tips
You can substitute beef or chicken if desired.

Pure maple syrup is a must for this recipe.

Make ahead
Complete to the end of Step 2. Refrigerate until needed.

Serve with...
Horseradish dip, tonkatsu sauce, red pepper aïoli.

Pork Satay

	Marinade		
Serves 4	2	cloves garlic, minced	2
	2 tbsp	natural crunchy peanut butter	25 mL
Crunchy peanut butter adds dimension to this satay recipe.	1 tbsp	freshly squeezed lime juice	15 mL
	1 tsp	packed brown sugar	5 mL
	½ tsp	ground coriander	2 mL
Tip	½ tsp	ground cumin	2 mL
Substitute boneless skinless chicken breast for the pork.	¼ tsp	hot pepper flakes	1 mL
	½ cup	soy sauce	125 mL
Make ahead	1 lb	pork tenderloin, thinly sliced and cut into 1-inch (2.5 cm) strips	500 g
Complete to the end of Step 2. Refrigerate until needed.		Oil for fondue	

Marinade: In a bowl, combine garlic, peanut butter, lime juice, brown sugar, coriander, cumin and hot pepper flakes. Mix well. Gradually whisk in soy sauce.

Serve with...
Tonkatsu sauce, tomato curry sauce, Asian dipping sauce.

1. *Marinade:* In a bowl, combine garlic, peanut butter, lime juice, brown sugar, coriander, cumin and hot pepper flakes. Mix well. Gradually whisk in soy sauce.

2. In a shallow casserole, pour marinade over pork, tossing to coat well. Cover and refrigerate for at least 1 hour.

3. Remove pork strips from marinade, shaking off any excess. Pat dry with a paper towel. Roll up strips and set aside on a platter.

4. In a saucepan, heat oil to 375°F (190°C) and transfer to fondue pot (or heat oil in an electric fondue). Do not fill fondue pot more than half full.

5. Spear rolled pork with fondue fork and fondue for 1 to 2 minutes or until cooked to desired doneness.

Pork Vindaloo

Marinade

2 tbsp	water	25 mL
2 tbsp	vinegar	25 mL
2	cloves garlic, minced	2
2 tsp	garam masala	10 mL
2 tsp	packed brown sugar	10 mL
1 tsp	minced gingerroot	5 mL
1 tsp	hot pepper flakes	5 mL
1 tsp	salt	5 mL
1 tsp	whole cumin seeds (optional)	5 mL
1 lb	pork tenderloin, cut into 1-inch (2.5 cm) cubes	500 g
	Oil for fondue	

1. *Marinade:* In a food processor, combine water, vinegar, garlic, garam masala, brown sugar, ginger, hot pepper flakes, salt and, if using, cumin; process to a smooth paste.

2. In a shallow casserole, spread paste over pork, tossing to coat well. Cover and refrigerate for at least 1 hour.

3. In a saucepan, heat oil to 375°F (190°C) and transfer to fondue pot (or heat oil in an electric fondue). Do not fill fondue pot more than half full.

4. Spear pork on fondue fork and fondue 1 to 2 minutes or until cooked to desired doneness.

Serves 4

Tip
Garam masala is a mixture of ground Asian spices — typically coriander, cumin, cardamom seeds, black peppercorns, cinnamon, whole cloves and whole nutmeg. You can find it in larger supermarkets and at Asian grocery stores.

Make ahead
Complete to the end of Step 2. Refrigerate until needed.

Serve with...
Sweet-and-sour sauce, Thai peanut sauce, mint yogurt dip.

Tonkatsu — Japanese Pork Cutlets

Tonkatsu is typically served over thinly sliced cabbage, soaked in cold water to soften. It is accompanied with tonkatsu sauce (see recipe, page 254), which is sprinkled over both the cabbage and the pork.

Tip
You can substitute chicken or turkey cutlets for the pork.

Make ahead
Complete to the end of Step 5. Refrigerate until needed.

Serve with...
Tonkatsu sauce, lemon wedges, Asian dipping sauce, wasabi mayonnaise.

1 lb	pork cutlets, cut into 1-inch (2.5 cm) strips	500 g
	Salt and freshly ground black pepper to taste	
½ cup	all-purpose flour	125 mL
1	egg	1
½ cup	panko crumbs or dry bread crumbs	125 mL
	Oil for fondue	

1. Sprinkle pork with salt and pepper. Refrigerate for up to 1 hour, allowing it to tenderize.

2. In a bowl, place flour.

3. In a second bowl, beat egg.

4. In a third bowl, place panko crumbs.

5. Dip pork slices one at a time in flour, then egg, then panko crumbs. Set breaded pork on a platter.

6. In a saucepan, heat oil to 375°F (190°C) and transfer to fondue pot (or heat oil in an electric fondue). Do not fill fondue pot more than half full.

7. Spear breaded pork with fondue fork and fondue for 1 to 2 minutes or until golden brown.

Dijon Rosemary Lamb Fondue

Marinade

¼ cup	Dijon mustard	50 mL
2 tbsp	white wine vinegar	25 mL
1 tbsp	chopped fresh rosemary	15 mL
1 tbsp	dried onion flakes	15 mL
1 tsp	garlic powder	5 mL
	Salt and freshly ground black pepper to taste	
1 lb	loin or leg of lamb, cut into 1-inch (2.5 cm) cubes	500 g
	Oil for fondue	

1. *Marinade:* In a bowl, combine mustard, vinegar, rosemary, onion flakes, garlic powder, salt and pepper. Mix well.

2. In a shallow casserole, pour marinade over lamb, tossing to coat well. Cover and refrigerate for at least 1 hour.

3. In a saucepan, heat oil to 375°F (190°C) and transfer to fondue pot (or heat oil in an electric fondue). Do not fill fondue pot more than half full.

4. Spear lamb cube with fondue fork and fondue for 1 to 2 minutes or until cooked to desired doneness.

Serves 4

Tip
Fresh rosemary takes this fondue up a notch. If it is not available, use 1 to 1½ tsp (5 to 7 mL) dried rosemary.

Make ahead
Complete to the end of Step 2. Refrigerate until needed.

Serve with...
Tzatziki, gremolata, roasted red pepper dip.

Chicken and Sausage Bites

Serves 4 to 6

Tip
Slice chicken breasts horizontally to cut into scallops or ask the butcher for scallops (or scaloppine).

Make ahead
Complete to the end of Step 4. Refrigerate. Bring to room temperature for 20 minutes before fonduing in oil.

Serve with...
Hot mustard, plum sauce, horseradish dip, honey dill dip.

1 lb	boneless skinless chicken breasts, cut into scallops	500 g
8 oz	Italian sausage, casings removed, meat crumbled	250 g
1 cup	coarsely ground soda cracker crumbs	250 mL
1 tsp	dried Italian seasoning	5 mL
½ tsp	garlic powder	2 mL
	Salt and freshly ground black pepper to taste	
2	eggs	2
	Oil for fondue	

1. Lay a chicken scallop on work surface. Spread with a couple of tablespoons of crumbled sausage meat. Roll up scallop jelly-roll fashion, then slice into 1-inch (2.5 cm) pieces, pinching ends of each piece to enclose chicken around the sausage.

2. In a bowl, combine soda cracker crumbs, dried Italian seasoning, garlic powder, salt and pepper.

3. In another bowl, beat eggs.

4. Dip each chicken piece in egg, then in crumb mixture, making sure pieces are thoroughly coated.

5. In a saucepan, heat oil to 375°F (190°C) and transfer to fondue pot (or heat oil in an electric fondue). Do not fill fondue pot more than half full.

6. Spear chicken piece with fondue fork and fondue for 1 to 2 minutes or until golden brown.

Chicken Nuggets

¼ cup	all-purpose flour	50 mL
¼ tsp	garlic powder	1 mL
	Salt and freshly ground black pepper to taste	
2	eggs	2
1 cup	dry bread crumbs	250 mL
½ tsp	dry mustard	2 mL
½ tsp	paprika	2 mL
Pinch	cayenne pepper	Pinch
1 lb	boneless skinless chicken breasts, cut into 1-inch (2.5 cm) cubes	500 g
	Oil for fondue	

1. In a bowl, combine flour, garlic powder, salt and black pepper.

2. In a second bowl, beat eggs.

3. In a third bowl, combine bread crumbs with mustard, paprika and cayenne.

4. Dip chicken cubes one at a time in flour mixture, then egg, then bread crumbs. Set breaded chicken aside on platter.

5. In a saucepan, heat oil to 375°F (190°C) and transfer to fondue pot (or heat oil in an electric fondue). Do not fill fondue pot more than half full.

6. Spear chicken nugget on fondue fork and fondue for 1 to 2 minutes or until golden brown.

Serves 4

Reminiscent of chicken fingers, this recipe is always a favorite with kids.

Tips
In place of bread crumbs, use finely processed or crushed soda crackers.

For a different flavor, use boneless skinless turkey breast.

Make ahead
Complete to the end of Step 4. Refrigerate. Bring to room temperature for 20 minutes before fonduing in oil.

Serve with...
Sweet-and-sour sauce, honey dill sauce, barbecue sauce.

Italian Breaded Chicken

Serves 4

Tip

Pistachios, a relative of cashews, are most often sold as dried nuts. Pistachios provide a rich source of dietary fiber and are also an excellent source of potassium, magnesium, copper and thiamine.

Make ahead

Complete to the end of Step 3. Refrigerate. Bring to room temperature for 20 minutes before fonduing in oil.

Serve with...

Garlic aïoli, zesty mayonnaise, lemon dill dip, blue cheese dip.

2	cloves garlic, minced	2
2 tbsp	finely ground pistachio nuts	25 mL
1 cup	dry bread crumbs	250 mL
1 tsp	hot pepper flakes	5 mL
1 tsp	dried basil	5 mL
1 tsp	dried oregano	5 mL
1 tbsp	freshly grated Parmesan cheese (preferably Parmigiano-Reggiano)	15 mL
	Salt and freshly ground black pepper to taste	
2	eggs	2
1 lb	boneless skinless chicken breasts, cut into 1-inch (2.5 cm) cubes	500 g
	Oil for fondue	

1. In a food processor, combine garlic and pistachios; process to a fine mince. Transfer mixture to a bowl. Stir in bread crumbs and mix well. Season with hot pepper flakes, basil, oregano, salt and pepper. Stir in Parmesan cheese.

2. In another bowl, beat eggs.

3. Dip chicken pieces in eggs, then in bread crumb mixture. Transfer breaded chicken to a platter.

4. In a saucepan, heat oil to 375°F (190°C) and transfer to fondue pot (or heat oil in an electric fondue). Do not fill fondue pot more than half full.

5. Spear breaded chicken with fondue fork and fondue for 1 to 2 minutes or until cooked to desired doneness.

Lemon Chicken Oil Fondue

1 cup	all-purpose flour	250 mL
2 tsp	grated lemon zest	10 mL
1 tsp	dried oregano	5 mL
½ tsp	garlic powder	2 mL
½ tsp	lemon pepper	2 mL
¼ tsp	salt	1 mL
2	eggs	2
1 lb	boneless skinless chicken breasts, cut into 1-inch (2.5 cm) cubes	500 g
	Oil for fondue	

1. In a bowl, combine flour, lemon zest, oregano, garlic powder, lemon pepper and salt.

2. In another bowl, beat eggs.

3. Dip each chicken cube in beaten egg, then coat with flour mixture. Place coated chicken pieces on a baking sheet lined with waxed paper and refrigerate for 15 minutes.

4. Remove chicken pieces from refrigerator and repeat dipping/coating procedure.

5. In a saucepan, heat oil to 375°F (190°C) and transfer to fondue pot (or heat oil in an electric fondue). Do not fill fondue pot more than half full.

6. Spear chicken with fondue fork and fondue for 1 to 2 minutes or until cooked to desired doneness.

Serves 4

Tip
If chicken is still moist, do not dip in egg a second time, just recoat chicken with flour coating.

Make ahead
Complete to the end of Step 4. Refrigerate. Bring to room temperature for 20 minutes before fonduing in oil.

Serve with...
Honey dill dip, chili garlic sauce, sweet-and-sour sauce.

Spicy Southern Fried Chicken Nuggets

With their distinctive buttermilk flavor, these nuggets will remind you of southern fried chicken. Children love them!

Tip
Freshly grated Parmesan cheese (preferably Parmigiano-Reggiano) is essential in this recipe. The prepackaged variety just doesn't have the same flavor and texture.

Marinade

1 cup	buttermilk	250 mL
1 tbsp	Dijon mustard	15 mL
1 tsp	hot pepper sauce	5 mL
1	clove garlic, minced	1
	Salt and freshly ground black pepper to taste	
1 lb	boneless skinless chicken breasts, cut into ½-inch (1 cm) cubes	500 g
2 cups	dry bread crumbs	500 mL
¼ cup	all-purpose flour	50 mL
¼ cup	freshly grated Parmesan (preferably Parmigiano-Reggiano)	50 mL
2 tsp	chili powder	10 mL
2 tsp	dried thyme	10 mL
½ tsp	coarse salt	2 mL
¼ tsp	freshly ground black pepper	1 mL
	Oil for fondue	

1. *Marinade:* In a bowl, combine buttermilk, Dijon mustard, hot pepper sauce, garlic, salt and black pepper; mix well.

2. In a shallow casserole, pour marinade over chicken, tossing to coat well. Cover and refrigerate for at least 1 hour.

3. In another bowl, combine bread crumbs, flour, Parmesan, chili powder, thyme, salt and pepper.

4. Remove chicken from fridge and, one piece at a time, shake off excess marinade and dip in bread crumb mixture. Transfer breaded chicken pieces to a platter.

5. In a saucepan, heat oil to 375°F (190°C) and transfer to fondue pot (or heat oil in an electric fondue). Do not fill fondue pot more than half full.

6. Spear chicken on fondue fork and fondue about 2 minutes or until golden brown and crispy.

Fondue is the perfect cooking method in which to stretch your creative culinary spirit. You can adjust the spiciness of a marinade, coating or broth to suit your taste, devise your own accompaniments or serve sauces based on what you have in the house. In this recipe, you can replace the chili powder and thyme with your favorite herb/spice combination, such as a Cajun spice mix, curry powder, herbes de Provence or Italian seasoning.

Make ahead

Complete to the end of Step 4. Refrigerate. Bring to room temperature for 20 minutes before fonduing in oil.

Serve with...

Green salsa, sweet-and-sour sauce, honey dill dip, barbecue sauce, sweet mustard dip.

Zesty Lime Chicken

I like to add cooked leftovers of this recipe to fried rice the next day. The lime flavor is excellent!

Tip

If you happen to have fondue leftovers, don't despair! Just fondue the remaining uncooked meat, fish or chicken, then keep in the refrigerator for another use.

Make ahead

Complete to the end of Step 2. Refrigerate until needed.

Serve with...

Peanut sauce, mango salsa or chutney, tomato curry sauce, honey dill dip.

Marinade

¼ cup	olive oil	50 mL
¼ cup	dry white wine	50 mL
2 tsp	freshly squeezed lime juice	10 mL
1 tsp	finely minced lime zest	5 mL
1	clove garlic, minced	1
½ tsp	hot pepper flakes	2 mL
¼ tsp	granulated sugar	1 mL
	Salt and freshly ground black pepper to taste	
1 lb	boneless skinless chicken breasts, thinly sliced and cut into 1-inch (2.5 cm) strips	500 g
	Oil for fondue	

1. *Marinade:* In a bowl, combine oil, wine, lime juice, lime zest, garlic, hot pepper flakes, sugar, salt and black pepper; mix well.

2. In a shallow casserole, pour marinade over chicken, tossing to coat well. Cover and refrigerate for at least 1 hour.

3. In a saucepan, heat oil to 375°F (190°C) and transfer to fondue pot (or heat oil in an electric fondue). Do not fill fondue pot more than half full.

4. Spear chicken with fondue fork and fondue 1 to 2 minutes or until cooked through.

Turkey Meatball Fondue

1 lb	lean ground turkey	500 g
½ cup	fresh bread crumbs	125 mL
1	egg, beaten	1
2	cloves garlic, minced	2
1	shallot, minced	1
1 tbsp	chopped fresh parsley (or 1 tsp/5 mL dried)	15 mL
¼ tsp	dried thyme	1 mL
	Salt and freshly ground black pepper to taste	
	Oil for fondue	

1. In large bowl, combine turkey, bread crumbs, egg, garlic, shallot, parsley, thyme, salt and pepper. Mix well. Using your hands, form into 40 meatballs, each about 1 inch (2.5 cm) in diameter.

2. Place on a baking sheet or platter lined with waxed paper and serve immediately or refrigerate until just before required. If refrigerated, place on counter for 15 minutes and bring to room temperature before fonduing.

3. In a saucepan, heat oil to 375°F (190°C) and transfer to fondue pot (or heat oil in an electric fondue). Do not fill fondue pot more than half full.

4. Spear meatball with fondue fork and fondue for 4 minutes or until cooked through and no longer pink inside

Serves 4

Ground turkey has its own distinctive flavor — you can also serve the meatballs with cranberry sauce.

Tip
You can use ground chicken or beef in place of the ground turkey.

Make ahead
Complete to the end of Step 2.

Serve with...
Sweet-and-sour sauce, honey mustard, mango chutney.

Turkey Thyme

Tip

This fondue can also be cooked in broth.

Make ahead

Complete to the end of Step 2. Refrigerate until needed.

Serve with...

Honey dill dip, sweet mustard dip, horseradish dip, lemon sauce.

1 lb	boneless skinless turkey breast, thinly sliced and cut into 1-inch (2.5 cm) strips	500 g
1 tsp	dried thyme	5 mL
½ tsp	garlic powder	2 mL
	Salt and freshly ground black pepper to taste	
	Oil for fondue	

1. Lay turkey pieces flat in a shallow casserole; season with thyme, garlic powder, salt and pepper. Cover and refrigerate for at least 1 hour.

2. Remove strips from refrigerator. Roll each piece and transfer to a platter.

3. In a saucepan, heat oil to 375°F (190°C) and transfer to fondue pot (or heat oil in an electric fondue). Do not fill fondue pot more than half full.

4. Spear turkey roll with fondue fork and and fondue for 1 to 2 minutes or until cooked through.

Bacon-Wrapped Scallop Fondue

12 oz	scallops	750 g
1 lb	sliced bacon, each slice cut into thirds	500 g
	Oil for fondue	

1. Wrap a scallop with a piece of bacon; secure with a toothpick and place on platter. Continue until all scallops are wrapped in bacon.

2. In a saucepan, heat oil to 375°F (190°C) and transfer to fondue pot (or heat oil in an electric fondue). Do not fill fondue pot more than half full. Before using, allow oil to cool slightly (see tip, at right) to 350°F (180°C).

3. Spear bacon-wrapped scallop with fondue fork and remove toothpick. Fondue in moderately hot oil for 3 to 5 minutes or until bacon starts to brown.

Serves 4

Tip
Bacon is prone to spatter when placed in hot oil, so you will need to reduce the temperature of the oil for this fondue recipe. Do this by lowering the flame on a conventional fondue pot or the thermostat on an electric pot. When testing to see if the oil is at the right temperature, remember to do so at a safe distance (just in case the bacon spatters).

Make ahead
Complete to the end of Step 1. Refrigerate until needed.

Serve with...
Shrimp cocktail dip, mustard and mayonnaise sauce, and side dishes of pasta and spinach salad.

Coconut Shrimp

Tip

Mince the coconut finely so it will adhere better to the shrimp.

For extra zing, add 1/4 tsp (1 mL) cayenne pepper to coconut.

Battered meat, poultry or seafood should always be brought to room temperature before fonduing.

Make ahead

Complete to the end of Step 4. Refrigerate. Bring to room temperature for 20 minutes before fonduing in oil.

Serve with...

Mango salsa or chutney, plum sauce, Asian dipping sauce, lemon sauce, salsa verde.

1/4 cup	coconut milk	50 mL
2 tbsp	freshly squeezed lime juice	25 mL
1/2 cup	dry bread crumbs	125 mL
1 tsp	curry powder	5 mL
	Salt and freshly ground black pepper to taste	
1 lb	shrimp, peeled and deveined	500 g
1	egg	1
1/2 cup	shredded unsweetened coconut	125 mL
	Oil for fondue	

1. In a bowl, combine coconut milk and lime juice.

2. In a second bowl, combine bread crumbs with curry powder, salt and pepper.

3. Dip shrimp one at a time in coconut milk, then coat in bread crumbs. Place breaded shrimp on a platter and refrigerate for at least 15 minutes.

4. In a third bowl, beat egg. Place coconut on a plate. Dip shrimp in beaten egg, then roll in coconut until thoroughly coated.

5. In a saucepan, heat oil to 375°F (190°C) and transfer to fondue pot (or heat oil in an electric fondue). Do not fill fondue pot more than half full.

6. Spear shrimp on fondue fork and fondue for 1 to 2 minutes or until golden brown.

Cornmeal-Breaded Shrimp

½ cup	cornmeal	125 mL
¾ tsp	paprika	4 mL
½ tsp	garlic powder	2 mL
¼ tsp	hot pepper flakes	1 mL
¼ tsp	cayenne pepper	1 mL
¼ tsp	ground coriander	1 mL
	Salt and freshly ground black pepper to taste	
1 lb	shrimp, peeled and deveined	500 g
	Oil for fondue	

1. In a bowl, combine cornmeal, paprika, garlic powder, hot pepper flakes, cayenne pepper, coriander, salt and black pepper.

2. Rinse shrimp under warm water. Dip one at a time in cornmeal mixture, coating on all sides. Place breaded shrimp on platter decorated with cilantro sprigs and lemon slices.

3. In a saucepan, heat oil to 375°F (190°C) and transfer to fondue pot (or heat oil in an electric fondue). Do not fill fondue pot more than half full.

4. Spear shrimp on fondue fork and fondue for 1 to 2 minutes or until golden brown.

Serves 4

Cornmeal gives a new twist and texture to breaded shrimp.

Tip
You can also use this coating as a breading for fried fish — it's excellent on pickerel.

Make ahead
Complete to the end of Step 2. Refrigerate. Bring to room temperature for 20 minutes before fonduing in oil.

Serve with...
Salsa verde, shrimp cocktail sauce, honey dill sauce.

Hemp Seed–Encrusted Shrimp

Serves 4

As well as giving the shrimp a nice smoky flavor, hemp seed is a nutraceutical — full of healthy omega-3 and omega-6 fatty acids.

Tip
Hemp seed is available at many health food and specialty food stores.

Make ahead
Complete to the end of Step 3. Refrigerate. Bring to room temperature for 20 minutes before fonduing in oil.

Serve with...
Shrimp cocktail sauce, zesty mayonnaise, salsa verde, lemon dill dip.

1 cup	hemp seeds (see tip, at left)	250 mL
1 tsp	paprika	5 mL
1 tsp	ground turmeric	5 mL
1 tsp	garlic powder	5 mL
½ tsp	cayenne pepper	2 mL
2	eggs	2
1 lb	shrimp, peeled and deveined	500 g
	Oil for fondue	

1. In a bowl, combine hemp seeds, paprika, turmeric, garlic powder and cayenne pepper.

2. In another bowl, beat eggs.

3. Dip shrimp one at a time into eggs, then coat with hemp seed mixture.

4. In a saucepan, heat oil to 375°F (190°C) and transfer to fondue pot (or heat oil in an electric fondue). Do not fill fondue pot more than half full.

5. Spear shrimp with fondue fork and fondue for 1 to 2 minutes or until browned.

Shrimp in Beer Batter

⅓ cup	all-purpose flour	75 mL
¼ tsp	salt	1 mL
Pinch	freshly ground black pepper	Pinch
2 tsp	Cajun seasoning (optional)	10 mL
4 tsp	butter, melted	20 mL
1	whole egg, beaten	1
½ cup	beer	125 mL
1	egg white	1
1 lb	shrimp, peeled and deveined	500 g
	Oil for fondue	

1. In a bowl, sift together flour and salt. Sprinkle in pepper and Cajun seasoning (if using), stirring well. Whisk in butter and egg until blended. Slowly whisk in beer until smooth. Set aside in a warm place and let stand for 1 hour.

2. Beat egg white until stiff peaks form; fold into batter.

3. In a saucepan, heat oil to 375°F (190°C) and transfer to fondue pot (or heat oil in an electric fondue). Do not fill fondue pot more than half full.

4. Dip shrimp in batter immediately before you are ready to fondue. Spear shrimp with fondue fork and fondue for 1 to 2 minutes or until golden brown.

Serves 4 to 6

Tips

You can also use beer batter to coat chunks of fish or other seafood, such as squid.

This amount of batter is enough to coat 1 lb (500 g) of tiger shrimp.

The Cajun seasoning adds zing to the batter.

Make ahead

It's best to prepare the beer batter and coat the shrimp just before serving.

Serve with...

Tzatziki, spicy sesame mayonnaise, shrimp cocktail sauce.

Cottage Cheese Fritters

Serves 4

Reminiscent of cheese blintzes or latkes, this recipe is perfect for dessert or brunch.

Tips

The recipe may be doubled.

If you can't find dry cottage cheese, use farmer cheese or 1% cottage cheese. Drain 1% cottage cheese in cheesecloth, then dry with a paper towel.

Make ahead

Complete to the end of Step 2. Refrigerate until ready to fondue.

Serve with...

Sour cream and frozen strawberries.

1¼ cups	dry cottage cheese	300 mL
½ cup	all-purpose flour, divided	125 mL
¼ cup	sour cream	50 mL
1	egg	1
1 tbsp	granulated sugar	15 mL
1 tbsp	butter, melted	15 mL
¼ tsp	salt	1 mL
	Oil for fondue	

1. In a food processor, process cottage cheese, ¼ cup (50 mL) of the flour, sour cream, egg, sugar, butter and salt until just combined. Do not overprocess. Using your hands, form into 16 balls, each about 1 inch (2.5 cm) in diameter.

2. Place on a baking sheet lined with waxed paper. Refrigerate for at least 1 hour.

3. Place the remaining ¼ cup (50 mL) flour in a bowl. Coat each cottage cheese ball in flour.

4. In a saucepan, heat oil to 375°F (190°C) and transfer to fondue pot (or heat oil in an electric fondue). Do not fill fondue pot more than half full.

5. Spear cheese fritters with fondue fork and fondue for 1 to 2 minutes or until golden brown and done in the center.

Mozzarella Cubes

1 cup	dry bread crumbs	250 mL
1 tsp	garlic powder	5 mL
1 tsp	dried basil	5 mL
1 tsp	dried oregano	5 mL
½ tsp	dried onion flakes	2 mL
¼ tsp	salt	1 mL
¼ tsp	freshly ground black pepper	1 mL
2	eggs	2
¼ cup	all-purpose flour	50 mL
8 oz	mozzarella cheese, cubed	250 g
	Oil for fondue	

1. In a bowl, combine bread crumbs, garlic powder, basil, oregano, onion flakes, salt and pepper.

2. In another bowl, beat eggs. Place flour on a plate or in a shallow bowl. Dip mozzarella cube in egg, flour, in egg again and finally in seasoned bread crumbs.

3. Place breaded cubes on a baking sheet lined with waxed paper and refrigerate for 30 minutes to set. Remove from refrigerator and bring to room temperature.

4. In a saucepan, heat oil to 375°F (190°C) and transfer to fondue pot (or heat oil in an electric fondue). Do not fill fondue pot more than half full.

5. Place one or two mozzarella cubes in Chinese basket (see tip, at right). Lower into oil fondue and fondue about 30 seconds or until golden brown. Remove, pat excess oil off with a paper towel and serve.

Serves 4 to 6

Tips
When mozzarella cubes are cold, the crumbs do not stick as well to the cheese. Bring to room temperature before fonduing.

A Chinese basket is a long-handled utensil with a wire basket on the end — ideal for dipping into oil fondues. Place one or two cubes in basket, lower into hot oil and fondue for about 30 seconds. Drain on paper towel and serve.

Make ahead
Complete to the end of Step 3. Refrigerate. Bring to room temperature for 20 minutes before fonduing in oil.

Serve with...
Honey dill dip, chili garlic sauce, mint yogurt dip, roasted red pepper dip, tomato curry sauce.

Falafel

1	package (12 oz/397 g) falafel mix	1
½ tsp	ground cumin	2 mL
¼ tsp	hot pepper flakes	1 mL
1½ cups	water	375 mL
	Oil for fondue	

1. In bowl, combine falafel mix, cumin, hot pepper flakes and water. Mix well. Let stand at room temperature for 1 hour.

2. Using your hands, form falafel mixture into 72 balls, each about 1 inch (2.5 cm) in diameter. Refrigerate for at least 30 minutes.

3. In a saucepan, heat oil to 375°F (190°C) and transfer to fondue pot (or heat oil in an electric fondue). Do not fill fondue pot more than half full.

4. When ready to fondue, remove a quarter of the falafel balls at a time, keeping the remainder chilled until needed. Spear balls with fondue fork and fondue for 2 to 3 minutes or until cooked through and browned.

Jalapeño Poppers

1 lb	jalapeño peppers (about 16)	500 g
5 oz	cream cheese, softened	150 g
2 tbsp	freshly squeezed lemon juice	25 mL
2	cloves garlic, minced	2
¼ tsp	onion powder	1 mL
¼ tsp	hot pepper flakes	1 mL
¼ tsp	salt	1 mL
¼ tsp	freshly ground black pepper	1 mL
	Oil for fondue	

1. With a sharp knife, cut the top off each jalapeño and carefully remove seeds and membranes.

2. In a small bowl, combine cream cheese, lemon juice, garlic, onion powder, hot pepper flakes, salt and black pepper. Mix well.

3. Fill each jalapeño with cream cheese mixture. Refrigerate for at least 30 minutes.

4. In a saucepan, heat oil to 375°F (190°C) and transfer to fondue pot (or heat oil in an electric fondue). Do not fill fondue pot more than half full.

5. Spear jalapeño poppers with fondue fork and fondue for 2 to 3 minutes or until peppers are softened.

Serve jalapeño poppers as appetizers; you should have about 4 per person.

Tips
The seeds in hot peppers provide much of the heat, so be sure to remove all of them before stuffing the peppers.

A large variety of hot chili peppers are available today, and any of them can be substituted for the jalapeños in this recipe. Just be wary of red hot peppers — they are fiery.

Add 2 tbsp (25 mL) finely chopped pine nuts and 1 tbsp (15 mL) chopped fresh basil to the cream cheese filling for added pesto-inspired flavor.

Make ahead
Complete to the end of Step 3. Refrigerate until needed.

Serve with...
Tzatziki, guacamole, fresh tomato salsa.

Tempura Vegetables

Recipe tester Cheryl Warkentin supplied this recipe for tempura, a favorite in her house. It's especially good served with Tomato Curry Sauce (see recipe, page 256).

Tip
Use tempura batter to coat tiger shrimp or sweet potatoes (partially cooked). This batter recipe is enough to coat 1 lb (500 g) of tiger shrimp.

Make ahead
Steam or parboil vegetables until tender-crisp. It's best to prepare the tempura batter and coat the vegetables or shrimp just before serving.

Serve with...
Asian dipping sauce, wasabi mayonnaise, tomato curry sauce.

3 cups	chopped vegetables (such as cauliflower and broccoli florets, red onions, bell peppers and mushrooms)	750 mL
1 cup	all-purpose flour	250 mL
1 tbsp	curry powder (optional)	15 mL
¼ tsp	salt	1 mL
2	eggs	2
6 tbsp	water	90 mL
3 tbsp	olive oil	45 mL
	Oil for fondue	

1. Steam or parboil vegetables for about 5 minutes or until tender-crisp. Refresh under cold water. Drain and set aside.

2. In a bowl, with an electric mixer, combine flour, curry powder (if using), salt, eggs, water and oil. Beat until well blended. Dip cauliflower florets in batter. Set aside on platter.

3. In a saucepan, heat oil to 375°F (190°C) and transfer to fondue pot (or heat oil in an electric fondue). Do not fill fondue pot more than half full.

4. Spear tempura floret with fondue fork and fondue for 30 seconds to 1 minute or until golden brown.

"Fried" Mars Bar Fondue

12	mini Mars bars (or 3 full-size Mars bars, cut into quarters)	12
	Oil for fondue	

1. Refrigerate Mars bars overnight or for at least 3 hours. Unwrap.

2. In a saucepan, heat oil to 375°F (190°C) and transfer to fondue pot (or heat oil in an electric fondue). Do not fill fondue pot more than half full.

3. Spear Mars bars with fondue fork and fondue for 30 seconds or until just starting to soften. Let cool slightly before eating.

Serves 4 to 6

This is the perfect fondue to experiment with after Halloween.

Make ahead
Cut up fruit to serve alongside.

Serve with...
Fruit... and a big glass of milk.

Broth fondues

Broth fondues

Ingredients

B Y VARYING COMBINATIONS of different broths and foods to be cooked in them, broth fondues offer an almost endless number of possibilities. Many are low in fat (at least, compared with cheese or oil fondues) and, as you'll see in this chapter, incorporate a wide range of international cooking styles.

The first decision to be made is whether to use a homemade or prepared base for the broth. Homemade is the most inexpensive and flavorful — and, if you make large batches and freeze them in fondue-sized portions for later use, quite convenient. Still, there are many occasions where there just isn't time to make a broth from scratch. In such cases, canned chicken and beef broth can be substituted. Most recipes in this chapter call for 5 cups (1.25 L) broth. Feel free to use packaged products labeled "broth" or "stock"; regardless of what the label says, they are all technically broth. Make sure to check whether the product is condensed; if it is, follow the directions on the label to dilute it.

High-quality cuts like beef tenderloin, pork tenderloin, lamb loin, chicken breast and turkey breast are the top choices for broth fondue. Deveined and peeled shrimp, scallops, and meaty fish like tuna or halibut are also good dippers into broth. Because broth fondues cook at a much lower temperature than oil, meat should be sliced very thinly, in strips 1 inch (2.5 cm) long, and rolled individually for a pleasant presentation and to make spearing easier.

Vegetables and noodles star in many broth fondues, especially those styled along the lines of Asian hot pots. Seek out baby bok choy, bamboo shoots, bean sprouts, broccoli florets, cauliflower florets, mushrooms, peppers, green onions and spinach; all make excellent dippers.

In the fondue pot

THE PROCEDURE FOR PREPARING a broth fondue is not unlike that used for an oil fondue. Broth is boiled in a saucepan on the stove and then transferred to the fondue pot. The alcohol burner is then lit with a match and the flame adjusted with the movable handle to produce a steady simmer for the broth.

In broth fondues, meat takes approximately 3 to 5 minutes to cook; chicken and fish require 2 to 4 minutes, depending on personal taste. The broth in the fondue pot should be simmering over a medium flame (not boiling) during the course of the fondue.

Broth fondue recipes, in particular, do not have to be followed as stringently as dessert or cheese fondues. Use whatever vegetables you have on hand for dippers, and take liberties to spice up the broth or make it milder to suit your palate.

Serving the fondue

AS WITH AN OIL FONDUE, plan on approximately 4 to 6 oz (125 to 175 g) per person for a main-course meat or seafood fondue with other side dishes. Guests with larger appetites will require 6 to 8 oz (175 to 250 g).

One of the joys of broth fondues is the ability to make a scrumptious soup when nearly all of the meat and vegetables have been fondued. Simply add the remaining meat and vegetables to the fondue pot. In the meantime, soak rice stick noodles for 15 minutes in warm water. Drain and add to fondue pot. Simmer together for 5 to 10 minutes to allow flavors to blend. A Chinese basket works well for divvying up the vegetables, meat or seafood into individual soup bowls. Then ladle the broth and noodles into bowl and enjoy as a fondue closer.

Rice stick or rice vermicelli noodles, Chinese egg noodles, or bean thread noodles harmonize with broth fondues. Prepare noodles according to directions just before serving. Many Asian noodles require reconstituting for 15 minutes in warm water; they are then drained, snipped with kitchen shears (if desired) and served. Chinese egg noodles must be boiled for 5 to 10 minutes, then drained.

Beef Broth

Makes 12 to 16 cups (3 to 4 L)

Tips

To slice onion (without slicing yourself!), cut onion in half vertically, then place flat-side down onto cutting board and proceed with slicing; repeat with second half.

To simplify their removal at the end of cooking, enclose the whole cloves, bay leaf and black peppercorns in a cheesecloth bag.

Make ahead

Chop onion, peel and slice carrots, slice celery and chop parsley.

3 lbs	meaty beef bones (such as shank or short ribs)	1.5 kg
1	large onion, peeled and chopped	1
2	cloves garlic, halved	2
2	carrots, peeled and sliced	2
2	stalks celery, sliced	2
2	whole cloves	2
1	bay leaf	1
2 tsp	salt	10 mL
8	black peppercorns	8
$\frac{1}{2}$ cup	chopped fresh parsley (leaves and stems)	125 mL
12 to 16 cups	water	3 to 4 L

1. In a large stockpot or Dutch oven, combine all ingredients, ensuring vegetables and meat bones are well covered with water. Cover and bring to a boil. Reduce heat and simmer for $1\frac{1}{2}$ to 2 hours, stirring occasionally and skimming off any foam that rises to the surface. After 1 hour, taste and add salt if necessary.

2. Remove bones and strain stock through a sieve lined with cheesecloth, discarding solids. Allow stock to cool, then refrigerate. Once chilled, remove congealed fat from surface. Portion stock in $2\frac{1}{2}$- to 3-cup (625 to 750 mL) portions for use in fondues. Freeze if desired.

Chicken Broth

3 lbs	chicken, whole or cut up	1.5 kg
12 to 16 cups	water	3 to 4 L
1	large onion, sliced	1
4	stalks celery (with leaves), cut into large chunks	4
3	carrots, peeled and cut into large chunks	3
1	parsnip, peeled and sliced into rounds	1
2	cloves garlic, minced	2
2 tsp	salt	5 mL
¾ tsp	freshly ground black pepper	4 mL
½ cup	chopped fresh parsley (leaves and stems)	125 mL
3	sprigs fresh dill (leaves and stems), chopped	3

1. In a large stockpot or Dutch oven, add water to cover chicken. Bring to a boil and cook, uncovered, for 10 minutes, occasionally skimming off any foam that rises to the surface. Add onion, celery, carrots, parsnip, garlic, salt and pepper. Return to a boil. Reduce heat to low, cover and simmer for 1 hour. Taste and season with additional salt and pepper as required. Add parsley and dill; cover and simmer for another 30 minutes.

2. Remove chicken and reserve for another use, if desired (see tip, at right). Strain stock through a sieve lined with cheesecloth, discarding solids. Allow stock to cool, then refrigerate. Once chilled, remove congealed fat from surface. Portion stock in 2½- to 3-cup (625 to 750 mL) portions for use in fondues. Freeze if desired.

Makes 12 to 16 cups (3 to 4 L)

Tips

Stewing hens, often found in the freezer section of the supermarket for a reasonable price, make tasty chicken broth.

The boiled chicken from the broth can be used for chicken salad, chicken fajitas or chicken sandwiches. Remove the skin and bones before serving boiled chicken in any dish.

For a darker color and more flavor, leave the skin on the onion.

Make ahead

Peel and slice all vegetables in advance.

Curry Chicken Broth

Makes **12 cups (3 L)**		

This flavorful curry broth makes an excellent fondue for beef, lamb, seafood, fish or chicken.

Tip
Try the curry broth as a soup at the end of the meal. Add any remaining meat or fish and your choice of noodles (cooked thin egg noodles or rice vermicelli). Simmer all ingredients together and enjoy this savory treat.

Make ahead
Prepare curry chicken broth early in the day, keeping 3 to 5 cups (750 mL to 1.25 L) to serve as fondue.

Serve with...
Various dipping sauces — such as mango chutney, green salsa, yogurt mint dip, chili garlic sauce — to accompany chicken, lamb or seafood cooked in this broth.

1 tbsp	vegetable oil	15 mL
1	onion, chopped	1
2 tsp	curry powder	10 mL
2	cloves garlic, minced	2
12 cups	water	3 L
3 lbs	chicken, cut into pieces	1.5 kg
2	carrots, peeled and sliced	2
2	stalks celery (with leaves), sliced	2
1 tbsp	grated gingerroot	15 mL
½ tsp	salt	2 mL
	Freshly ground black pepper to taste	

1. In a large stockpot or Dutch oven, heat oil over medium heat. Add onion and sauté for 3 minutes. Add curry powder and garlic; continue to sauté until onions and garlic are softened (but not browned). Add water, chicken, carrots, celery, ginger, salt and pepper. Bring to a boil. Reduce heat and simmer, covered and stirring occasionally, for 2 hours or until meat is tender. Taste after 1 hour and season with additional curry powder, salt and/or pepper if necessary.

2. Remove chicken and reserve for another use, if desired (see tip, page 127). Strain stock through a sieve lined with cheesecloth, discarding solids. Allow stock to cool, then refrigerate. Once chilled, remove congealed fat from surface. Portion stock in $2\frac{1}{2}$- to 3-cup (625 to 750 mL) portions for use in fondues. Freeze if desired.

Fish Broth

2 lbs	fish heads and bones (white-fleshed fish, gills removed), rinsed	1 kg
12 cups	water	3 L
1	large onion, unpeeled, sliced in rings	1
2	cloves garlic, halved	2
2	carrots, peeled and sliced	2
2	stalks celery and leaves, chopped	2
2	leeks (white parts only), sliced	2
½ cup	chopped fresh parsley (leaves and stems)	125 mL
1½ tsp	salt	7 mL
¼ tsp	granulated sugar	1 mL
8	black peppercorns	8
1	bay leaf	1
1	strip (1 inch/2.5 cm) lemon zest	1

1. In a large stockpot or Dutch oven, add water to cover fish. Add onion, garlic, carrots, celery, leeks, parsley, salt, sugar, peppercorns, bay leaf and lemon zest. Bring to a boil. Reduce heat and simmer, covered, for 45 minutes. Taste after 30 minutes and adjust seasoning if required.

2. Remove fish heads and bones. Strain stock through a sieve lined with cheesecloth, discarding solids. Allow stock to cool, then refrigerate. Portion stock in 2½- to 3-cup (625 to 750 mL) portions for use in fish or seafood fondues (do not use for other foods). Freeze if desired.

Makes 12 cups (3 L)

Tip
When you cook fish broth, the odor is often unpleasant. To counteract this, place a couple of cinnamon sticks in a small saucepan of water and simmer, uncovered, replenishing the water as required.

Variation
Asian fish stock: *To 4 cups (1 L) fish broth, add 1 tbsp (15 mL) miso paste, 2 tbsp (25 mL) sake, 1 tbsp (15 mL) grated gingerroot and 1 chopped green onion. Bring to a boil. Reduce heat and simmer, covered, for 15 minutes to allow flavors to blend. Transfer to fondue pot and use with Asian hot pot fondues.*

Make ahead
Slice and chop all vegetables.

Prepare lemon zest.

Vegetable Broth

Makes 12 to 16 cups (3 to 4 L)

Tips

The potato-peel liquid used in this recipe may sound peculiar, but it infuses the vegetable stock with unmatched flavor. Using parsley stems (the most flavorful part of the herb) is another important taste enhancer.

Use the vegetables called for here or substitute whatever you've got in your fridge. Avoid cabbage, cauliflower or broccoli, however, since they will overpower the broth with an unpleasantly strong flavor.

Make ahead

Prepare potato liquid (Step 1) in advance.

Chop onions, carrots, celery and parsley.

4	large potatoes	4
5 cups	water (approx.)	1.25 L
2 tsp	olive oil	10 mL
1	large onion, chopped	1
8	carrots, peeled and chopped	8
8	stalks celery (with leaves), chopped	8
1	zucchini (with peel), chopped	1
½ cup	diced sweet potato	125 mL
6	cloves garlic, halved	6
8 cups	water (approx.)	2 L
2 cups	chopped fresh parsley (leaves and stems)	500 mL
2 tsp	dried thyme	10 mL
1 tbsp	salt	15 mL
12	black peppercorns	12

1. Peel potatoes and transfer peelings to a medium saucepan. (Potatoes can be cooked separately and reserved for another use.) Cover peelings with water (adjust quantity of water if necessary; peelings should be well covered). Bring to a boil. Reduce heat and simmer, covered, for 1 hour. Strain liquid through a sieve, discarding solids. Set aside.

2. In large stockpot or Dutch oven, heat oil over medium heat. Add onions and sauté until softened and starting to brown. Add reserved potato-peel liquid, along with carrots, celery, zucchini, sweet potato and garlic. Pour in additional 8 cups (2 L) water, or whatever is necessary to cover vegetables by 1 inch (2.5 cm). Add parsley, thyme, salt and peppercorns. Bring to a boil. Reduce heat and simmer, covered, for 1½ hours.

3. Strain stock through a sieve lined with cheesecloth, discarding solids. Allow stock to cool, then refrigerate. Portion stock in 2½- to 3-cup (625 to 750 mL) portions for use in fondues. Freeze if desired.

Wild Mushroom and Leek Broth

1½ tbsp	olive oil	22 mL
2	leeks (white parts only), chopped	2
3	cloves garlic, minced	3
⅓ cup	chopped wild or exotic mushrooms (such as shiitake and portobello)	75 mL
	Salt and freshly ground black pepper to taste	
¼ cup	dry sherry	50 mL
5 cups	beef broth (store-bought or see recipe, page 126)	1.25 L

Makes 5 to 6 cups (1.25 to 1.5 L)

Tips

If you can't find any leeks, use onions instead.

For a more intense mushroom flavor, increase amount of wild mushrooms used.

Wash leeks thoroughly, separating layers to remove any dirt between them before using.

Make ahead

Wash and chop leeks, mince garlic and chop mushrooms.

1. In a nonstick skillet, heat oil over medium heat. Add leeks, garlic and wild mushrooms; sauté for about 5 minutes or until softened. Transfer mixture to a food processor. Add sherry and process on and off 2 or 3 times, just until vegetables are puréed.

2. Transfer processed vegetables to a medium saucepan. Add beef broth and bring to a boil. Cook for 1 minute, then reduce heat and simmer, stirring occasionally, for 3 minutes. Transfer broth to a fondue pot and use to cook chicken or beef.

Asian Fusion Beef

Serves 4

Tips
Roasted dried onion flakes pack more punch than the regular dried onion flakes. Look for them at specialty and bulk food stores.

If you can't find spicy mango chutney, add 1 tsp (5 mL) chili garlic paste to the marinade.

Make ahead
Prepare marinade in advance and marinate beef for several hours before the fondue meal.

Serve with...
Spicy sesame mayonnaise, tonkatsu sauce, Asian dipping sauce.

Marinade

3 tbsp	hoisin sauce	45 mL
3 tbsp	spicy mango chutney	45 mL
2 tbsp	freshly squeezed lemon juice	25 mL
1 tbsp	minced gingerroot	15 mL
1 tsp	roasted dried onion flakes	5 mL
1	clove garlic, minced	1
1 lb	flank steak or sirloin steak, thinly sliced and cut into 1-inch (2.5 cm) strips	500 g

Broth

5 cups	beef broth (store-bought or see recipe, page 126)	1.25 L

1. *Marinade:* In a bowl, whisk together hoisin sauce, chutney, lemon juice, ginger, onion flakes and garlic.

2. In a shallow casserole, cover beef strips with marinade, tossing to coat well. Cover and refrigerate for at least 1 hour.

3. *Broth:* In a large saucepan, bring beef broth to a boil. Immediately transfer to fondue pot, setting flame to keep at a simmer.

4. Remove beef strip from marinade, roll and spear with fondue fork. Fondue for 3 to 5 minutes or until cooked to desired doneness.

Beef Broth with Red Wine, Leeks and Wild Mushrooms

1 tbsp	olive oil	15 mL
1	leek (white part only), minced	1
½ cup	chopped fresh wild or exotic mushrooms (such as shiitake and portobello)	125 mL
5 cups	beef broth (store-bought or see recipe, page 126)	1.25 L
¾ cup	red wine	175 mL
1 tsp	dried thyme	5 mL
1 lb	filet mignon, thinly sliced and cut into 1-inch (2.5 cm) strips	500 g

1. In a large saucepan, heat oil over medium heat. Add leek and wild mushrooms; sauté for 3 minutes or until vegetables are softened but not browned.

2. Add beef broth, red wine and thyme. Bring to a boil. Reduce heat to low and simmer, covered, for 15 minutes to allow flavors to blend. Transfer to fondue pot.

3. Spear rolled strip of filet mignon with fondue fork. Cook in broth, set over a medium flame, for 3 to 5 minutes or according to personal preference.

Shiitake mushrooms, with their umbrella-shaped caps and tan gills, have a rich, woodsy flavor and meaty texture when cooked. Their tough stems are normally discarded, but you can include them here to add flavor to this stock.

Tips
Shiitake mushrooms should be stored in a paper bag in the refrigerator; they will keep for up to 14 days.

For easy slicing, slice filet mignon when the meat is cold. Cut against the grain into thin slices, each about 1 inch (2.5 cm) long. Roll each piece and set on a platter.

Make ahead
Wash and slice leek in advance.

Prepare any desired dipping sauces.

Serve with...
A variety of sauces, such as sweet mustard, horseradish mayonnaise, garlic aïoli or spicy hot pepper sauce.

Jamaican Spiced Beef Hot Pot

With plenty of zesty heat in both the marinade and the broth, this is one spicy fondue — so keep the cold drinks close at hand!

Tips

Cilantro is also known as coriander or Chinese parsley. It's one of the world's oldest known spices and was reportedly cultivated 3,500 years ago in Egypt. Cilantro is used extensively in the cuisines of Latin America, China, India and Thailand.

Like most hot pots, the broth in this fondue makes a wonderful soup once most of the meat has been cooked in it. When about a quarter of the meat is left, add it to the pot along with presoaked and drained rice stick noodles or preboiled noodles of your choice. Enjoy!

Marinade

2 tbsp	freshly squeezed lemon juice	25 mL
1 tbsp	chili powder	15 mL
1 tbsp	vegetable oil	15 mL
1 tbsp	water	15 mL
½ tsp	curry paste or powder	2 mL
1 lb	filet mignon, thinly sliced and cut into 1-inch (2.5 cm) strips	500 g

Broth

1 tbsp	vegetable oil	15 mL
1	onion, chopped	1
2	cloves garlic, minced	2
5 cups	beef broth (store-bought or see recipe, page 126)	1.25 L
2	green onions, minced	2
1 tsp	minced gingerroot	5 mL
½ tsp	ground cumin	2 mL
½ tsp	hot pepper flakes	2 mL
½ tsp	garam masala	2 mL
1 tbsp	chopped fresh cilantro	15 mL

1. *Marinade:* In a bowl, combine lemon juice, chili powder, oil, water and curry paste. Stir until well mixed, adding more water, 1 tbsp (15 mL) at a time, if too thick. (Marinade should be thick but pourable.)

2. In a shallow casserole, cover beef strips with marinade, tossing to coat well. Cover and refrigerate for at least 1 hour.

3. *Broth:* In a large saucepan, heat oil over medium heat. Add onion and garlic; sauté until softened. Add beef broth along with green onions, ginger, cumin, hot pepper flakes and garam masala. Reduce heat and simmer, covered, for 15 minutes to allow flavors to blend.

4. Add cilantro to broth. Taste and adjust seasonings as needed. Bring quickly to a boil over high heat; immediately transfer to fondue pot.

5. Remove beef strip from marinade, roll and spear with fondue fork. Fondue for 3 to 5 minutes or until cooked to desired doneness.

Make ahead

Prepare marinade in advance and marinate filet mignon strips for several hours prior to the fondue.

Prepare the broth up to the end of Step 3. Before dinner, add the cilantro and carry out the remaining steps.

Serve with...
Mango chutney, peanut sauce, chili vinegar.

Mushroom and Oxtail Broth Fondue

Tips

You can use top sirloin in place of beef tenderloin.

To turn this fondue into a meal, serve with a vegetable platter consisting of broccoli and cauliflower florets, slices of zucchini and chunks of red and green peppers. Fondue vegetables to desired doneness. When about one-quarter of the beef remains, add it and any remaining vegetables to fondue pot. Simmer for several minutes, then, if desired, add soaked and drained rice stick noodles or cooked pasta shells. Serve as a soup to end the meal.

Make ahead

Broth can be prepared in advance and then boiled on the stovetop prior to transferring to fondue pot.

Serve with...

Sweet-and-sour sauce, honey mustard, gremolata.

Broth

1 tbsp	olive oil	15 mL
2	onions, sliced	2
2	cloves garlic, minced	15 mL
1	portobello mushroom, chopped	1
1 cup	chopped oyster mushrooms	250 mL
1 tsp	truffle oil	5 mL
1	package (3 oz/76 g) oxtail soup mix	1
4½ cups	water	1.125 L
¼ cup	red wine	50 mL
1 tsp	Worcestershire sauce	5 mL
1	bay leaf	1
1 lb	beef tenderloin, thinly sliced and cut into 1-inch (2.5 cm) strips	500 g

1. *Broth:* In a large saucepan, heat olive oil over medium heat. Add onions and garlic; sauté until softened. Reduce heat to low and add portobello and oyster mushrooms and truffle oil; sauté until mushrooms are tender. Add oxtail soup mix, water, wine, Worcestershire sauce and bay leaf. Bring to a boil. Reduce heat and simmer, covered, for 15 minutes. If too thick, add up to ½ cup (125 mL) boiling water. Transfer to fondue pot, setting flame to keep at a simmer.

2. Spear beef strip with fondue fork. Fondue for 3 to 5 minutes or until cooked to desired doneness.

Quick Onion Broth with Beef

1 lb	beef tenderloin or flank steak, thinly sliced and cut into 1-inch (2.5 cm) strips	500 g
Broth		
1	package (1.4 oz/39 g) dry onion soup mix	1
4½ cups	water	1.125 L
¼ cup	chopped fresh parsley	50 mL
1 tbsp	red wine vinegar	15 mL
1 tsp	Worcestershire sauce	5 mL
¼ tsp	dried thyme	1 mL
¼ tsp	freshly ground black pepper	1 mL

1. Roll up strips of beef and place on a large serving platter. Cover and set aside.

2. *Broth:* In a large saucepan, combine onion soup mix, water, parsley, red wine vinegar, Worcestershire sauce, thyme and pepper. Bring to a boil. Reduce heat and simmer, covered, for 15 minutes. Immediately transfer to fondue pot, setting flame to keep at a simmer.

3. Spear beef roll with fondue fork. Fondue for 3 to 5 minutes or until cooked to desired doneness.

Serves 4

Tips
You can use loin or leg of lamb in place of beef tenderloin.

When you are finished cooking the meat, you can mimic French onion soup by ladling the remainder of the broth into individual bowls and adding croutons and grated Swiss cheese on top.

Make ahead
Broth can be prepared in advance and then boiled on the stovetop prior to transferring to fondue pot.

Serve with...
Chili garlic sauce, sweet mustard dip, horseradish dip.

Quick Asian Hot Pot

Tip

Cook Chinese egg noodles for about 8 minutes in boiling water. Drain and set aside until needed. You can also use rice stick or bean thread noodles in place of Chinese egg noodles. Prepare noodles immediately before required.

Make ahead

Broth can be prepared in advance and then boiled on the stovetop prior to transferring to fondue pot.

Slice meat.

Prepare vegetable platter.

Prepare dipping sauces.

Broth

5 cups	beef broth (store-bought or see recipe, page 126)	1.25 L
2	green onions, minced	2
2	cloves garlic, minced	2
4 to 6	shiitake mushrooms, chopped	4 to 6
2 tbsp	chopped fresh cilantro	25 mL
2 tbsp	minced gingerroot	25 mL
2 tbsp	Japanese soy sauce	25 mL

Vegetable platter

8	bok choy leaves, cut into 2-inch (5 cm) strips	8
2 oz	spinach leaves, cut into 1-inch (2.5 cm) strips	60 g
1	can (8 oz/227 mL) bamboo shoots, drained	1
2	green onions, chopped	2
1 cup	broccoli florets	250 mL
1 lb	beef tenderloin, thinly sliced and cut into 1-inch (2.5 cm) strips	500 g
4 oz	Chinese egg noodles, cooked	125 g

1. *Broth:* In a large saucepan over high heat, bring beef broth to a boil. Add green onions, garlic, mushrooms, cilantro, ginger and soy sauce. Reduce heat and simmer, covered, for 15 minutes to allow flavors to blend. Immediately transfer to fondue pot.

2. *Vegetable platter:* Decoratively arrange bok choy, spinach, bamboo shoots and green onions on a serving platter. Place broccoli florets on top.

3. Spear beef strip with fondue fork. Fondue for 3 to 5 minutes or until cooked to desired doneness. Dip in desired sauces. Spear broccoli florets and simmer in broth until tender-crisp.

4. When meat is all eaten, add remaining vegetables and cooked egg noodles to broth. Simmer together for about 3 to 5 minutes. Provide each guest with a soup bowl and ladle Asian hot pot soup into each bowl. A Chinese basket can be used to retrieve and divide vegetables among guests. Season soup with Mongolian Hot Pot Dipping Sauce (see recipe, page 255) or chili garlic sauce.

Serve with...
Wasabi mayonnaise, Mongolian hot pot dipping sauce, chili garlic sauce, Thai peanut sauce, Asian dipping sauce.

Mustard-Infused Beef Fondue

There are about 40 different species of mustard plant, each distinguished mainly by its seeds, which are used to prepare various forms of the popular condiment. Mustard greens are also edible.

Make ahead

Prepare marinade in advance and marinate meat for several hours prior to the fondue.

Serve with...

Honey dip, horseradish mayonnaise dip, blue cheese dip.

Marinade

2 tsp	dry mustard	10 mL
4 tsp	water	20 mL
¼ cup	Dijon mustard	50 mL
2 tsp	packed brown sugar	10 mL
1 tbsp	vegetable oil	15 mL
	Salt and freshly ground black pepper to taste	
1 lb	beef tenderloin, thinly sliced and cut into 1-inch (2.5 cm) strips	500 g

Broth

5 cups	beef broth (store-bought or see recipe, page 126)	1.25 L

1. *Marinade:* In a bowl, whisk together dry mustard and water until dissolved. Add Dijon mustard, brown sugar, oil, salt and pepper; mix until well combined.

2. In a shallow casserole, rub beef strips with marinade, being sure that all pieces are well coated. Cover and refrigerate for at least 1 hour.

3. *Broth:* In a large saucepan over high heat, bring beef broth to a boil. Immediately transfer to fondue pot, setting flame to keep at a simmer.

4. Remove beef strip from marinade, roll and spear with fondue fork. Fondue for 3 to 5 minutes or until cooked to desired doneness.

North African Beef Fondue

Marinade

2	cloves garlic	2
1	piece (1 inch/2.5 cm) gingerroot	1
¼ cup	water	50 mL
2 tbsp	chopped fresh parsley	25 mL
1 tbsp	olive oil	15 mL
4 tsp	ground pistachios	20 mL
1 tsp	seven-spice seasoning	5 mL
1 lb	flank steak or sirloin steak, thinly sliced and cut into 1-inch (2.5 cm) strips	500 g

Broth

5 cups	beef broth (store-bought or see recipe, page 126)	1.25 L

1. *Marinade:* In a food processor, mince garlic and ginger. Add water, parsley, oil, pistachios and seven-spice seasoning; process to form a paste.

2. In a shallow casserole, brush beef strips with marinade, making sure all pieces are well coated. Cover and refrigerate for at least 1 hour.

3. *Broth:* In a large saucepan, bring beef broth to a boil. Immediately transfer to fondue pot, setting flame to keep at a simmer.

4. Remove beef strip from marinade, roll and spear with fondue fork. Fondue for 3 to 5 minutes or until cooked to desired doneness.

Serves 4

Tip
Seven-spice seasoning (allspice, black pepper, cinnamon, ginger, mahlab, nutmeg and cloves) is popular in Middle Eastern and North African cuisine. It adds a unique spiced flavor to the beef.

Make ahead
Prepare marinade in advance and marinate beef for several hours before the fondue meal.

Serve with...
Cilantro coulis, hummus, hot pepper sauce.

Sukiyaki

Serves 4 to 6

Japanese sukiyaki usually consists of beef and vegetables braised in a spicy soy sauce and served with beaten egg yolk and steamed rice. The dish is traditionally prepared at the table — on a large skillet or hibachi. With this recipe, I've kept the braising (albeit in a skillet on the stove) and adapted it to the Asian hot pot method. Try this dish — it's worth the effort.

Tips

Soak bean thread vermicelli in hot water for 20 minutes. Drain and cut into small pieces before adding to fondue pot.

Instead of bean thread vermicelli, portion steamed rice into each individual bowl and top with vegetables, tofu, beef and broth.

Sukiyaki sauce

1 tbsp	granulated sugar	15 mL
½ cup	tamari soy sauce	125 mL
½ cup	beef broth (homemade or canned; see below)	125 mL
2 tbsp	sake	25 mL
2 tbsp	vegetable oil	25 mL
1 lb	beef tenderloin, thinly sliced and cut into 1-inch (2.5 cm) strips	500 g

Quick Asian broth

5 cups	beef broth (store-bought or see recipe, page 126)	1.25 L
1 tsp	minced gingerroot	5 mL
1	clove garlic, minced	1
½ cup	sukiyaki sauce (from above)	125 mL
1 cup	bean sprouts, rinsed, ends removed	250 mL
1 cup	halved mushrooms	250 mL
1	can (8 oz/227 mL) bamboo shoots, drained	1
6 oz	baby bok choy, sliced	175 g
6 oz	firm tofu, cubed	175 g
4 oz	bean thread vermicelli, soaked and drained	125 g
2	green onions, chopped	2

1. *Sukiyaki sauce:* In a bowl, whisk together sugar, soy sauce, beef broth and sake. Set aside.

2. In a skillet, heat oil over medium heat. Add beef and stir-fry about 2 minutes. Pour half of the sukiyaki sauce (approximately ½ cup/125 mL) over beef; stir-fry until cooked through. Transfer beef to a platter for table.

3. *Quick Asian broth:* In a large saucepan, combine beef broth, ginger, garlic and remaining $1/2$ cup (125 mL) sukiyaki sauce. Bring to a boil. Reduce heat and simmer for 15 minutes to allow flavors to blend.

4. Transfer broth to fondue pot, setting flame to keep at a simmer. Add bean sprouts, mushrooms, bamboo shoots, bok choy, tofu, vermicelli and green onions. Provide each guest with a soup bowl and ladle broth and noodles into each bowl. A Chinese basket can be used to retrieve and divide vegetables and tofu among guests. Top each bowl with slices of beef.

Make ahead

Prepare sukiyaki sauce. Use half to make quick Asian broth. Immediately prior to fondue, bring to a boil on stovetop, then transfer to fondue pot.

Slice up vegetables and tofu for platter.

Serve with...

Wasabi mayonnaise, Asian dipping sauce, tamari sauce.

Paella Fondue

Serves 4

This is one of my favorite fondues to serve company — it offers an exceptional experience with its distinctive flavor and unforgettable soup at the end of the meal.

Tips

Saffron, though expensive, is mandatory to replicate the paella flavor in this recipe — and you only need a few threads for its irreplaceable effect.

Serve with boneless chicken thighs, pepperoni sticks or cooked sausages, and shrimp for a real paella experience.

Make ahead

Broth can be prepared in advance and then boiled on the stovetop prior to transferring to fondue pot.

Serve with...

Gremolata, red pepper aïoli, cilantro coulis.

Broth

1 tbsp	olive oil	15 mL
1	onion, chopped	1
2	cloves garlic, minced	2
¼ cup	chopped green bell pepper	50 mL
¼ cup	chopped red bell pepper	50 mL
5 cups	beef broth (store-bought or see recipe, page 126)	1.25 L
1	can (28 oz/796 mL) Italian stewed tomatoes, with juice	1
1½ cups	dry white wine	375 mL
1	bay leaf	1
¼ cup	chopped fresh cilantro	50 mL
½ tsp	dried thyme	2 mL
¼ tsp	hot pepper flakes	1 mL
Pinch	crumbled saffron	Pinch
	Salt and freshly ground black pepper to taste	
1 lb	beef tenderloin, thinly sliced and cut into 1-inch (2.5 cm) strips	500 g

1. *Broth:* In a large saucepan, heat oil over medium heat. Add onion, garlic and red and green peppers; sauté until softened. Add beef broth, tomatoes, wine, bay leaf, cilantro, thyme, hot pepper flakes, saffron, salt and black pepper. Bring to a boil. Reduce heat and simmer, covered, for 30 minutes. If too thick, add up to ½ cup (125 mL) boiling water. Transfer to fondue pot, setting flame to keep at a simmer.

2. Spear beef strip with fondue fork and fondue for 3 to 5 minutes or until cooked to desired doneness.

Hawaiian Pork (page 96) with Mango Salsa (page 247)

Dijon Rosemary Lamb Fondue (page 101)

Coconut Shrimp (page 112)

Jalapeño Poppers (page 119)

Tempura Vegetables (page 120)

Beef Broth with Red Wine, Leeks and Wild Mushrooms (page 133)

Paella Fondue (page 144)

Italian Wedding Broth with Veal (page 149)

Spicy Beef Fondue

Marinade

2 tbsp	granulated sugar	25 mL
¼ cup	olive oil	50 mL
4	cloves garlic, minced	4
4 tsp	curry powder	20 mL
4 tsp	ground coriander	20 mL
1 tsp	ground cumin	5 mL
¼ tsp	ground cinnamon	1 mL
½ tsp	ground ginger	2 mL
½ tsp	salt	2 mL
	Freshly ground black pepper to taste	
1 lb	beef tenderloin or flank steak, thinly sliced and cut into 1-inch (2.5 cm) strips	500 g

Broth

5 cups	beef broth (store-bought or see recipe, page 126)	1.25 L

1. *Marinade:* In a bowl, whisk together sugar and olive oil. Add garlic, curry powder, coriander, cumin, cinnamon, ginger, salt and pepper. Stir well to form a paste.

2. In a shallow casserole, rub beef strips with marinade, being sure that all pieces are well coated. Cover and refrigerate for at least 1 hour.

3. *Broth:* In a large saucepan over high heat, bring beef broth to a boil. Immediately transfer to fondue pot, setting flame to keep at a simmer.

4. Remove beef strip from marinade, roll and spear with fondue fork. Fondue for 3 to 5 minutes or until cooked to desired doneness.

Tip

This delicious fondue can also be made with flank steak — a less expensive cut that, after marinating, becomes quite tender. Marinate flank steak for 2 to 8 hours. When slicing, be sure to cut across the grain.

Make ahead

Prepare marinade in advance and marinate beef tenderloin pieces for several hours before the fondue meal.

Serve with...

Plum sauce, sweet-and-sour sauce, garlic aïoli.

Teriyaki Beef Fondue

Tip

Try this recipe with boneless skinless chicken breasts instead of beef.

Make ahead

Prepare marinade in advance and marinate beef strips for several hours before the fondue meal.

Serve with...

Dijonnaise, Asian dipping sauce, sweet-and-sour sauce.

Marinade

3 tbsp	soy sauce	15 mL
1 tbsp	vegetable oil	15 mL
1 tbsp	water	15 mL
1 tbsp	liquid honey	15 mL
2 tsp	minced gingerroot	10 mL
1	clove garlic, minced	1
1 lb	beef tenderloin, thinly sliced and cut into 1-inch (2.5 cm) strips	500 g

Broth

5 cups	beef broth (store-bought or see recipe, page 126)	1.25 L
⅓ cup	soy sauce	75 mL
2 tbsp	packed brown sugar	25 mL
1 tbsp	cider vinegar	15 mL
1 tbsp	sake or dry sherry	15 mL
2	cloves garlic, minced	2
1 tbsp	minced gingerroot	15 mL

1. *Marinade:* In a bowl, whisk together soy sauce, oil, water, honey, ginger and garlic. Mix well.

2. In a shallow casserole, cover beef strips with marinade, tossing to coat well. Cover and refrigerate for at least 30 minutes.

3. *Broth:* In a large saucepan, combine beef broth with soy sauce, brown sugar, vinegar, sake, garlic and ginger. Bring to a boil. Reduce heat and simmer, covered, for 20 to 30 minutes. Transfer to fondue pot, setting flame to keep at a simmer.

4. Remove beef strip from marinade, roll and spear with fondue fork. Fondue for 3 to 5 minutes or until cooked to desired doneness.

Cocktail Franks

1	jar (8 oz/250 mL) grape jelly or seedless blackcurrant jelly	250 mL
1/3 cup	prepared mustard	75 mL
1 lb	cocktail franks or hot dogs cut diagonally into bite-size pieces	500 g

1. In a large saucepan over medium-low heat, melt together jelly and prepared mustard, stirring frequently, for approximately 5 minutes. Bring mixture to a boil and cook, stirring, for 1 minute or until mixture is reduced slightly. Immediately transfer to fondue pot, setting flame to keep at a simmer.

2. Spear franks with fondue fork and fondue for 5 minutes or until frank is bubbling.

Serves 4 to 6

This quick and easy recipe makes a super kid-friendly fondue. (My youngest son, Evan, loves it!) The hot dogs are swathed in the sweet sauce, so an additional dipping sauce is not necessary.

Make ahead

Since it's so straightforward, there's little advance work necessary! However, you can prepare the jelly-mustard sauce earlier in the day and then simply reheat on stove and transfer to fondue point once it has boiled for a minute or so.

Fondue à la Veal Parmesan

Serves 4

The broth in this recipe is more like a tomato sauce. You'll need to allow more time for it to cook the meat than you would for broth.

Make ahead

Broth can be prepared in advance and then boiled on the stovetop prior to transferring to fondue pot.

Serve with...

Lemon sauce, sweet mustard dip, pasta and steamed asparagus.

1 lb	veal scaloppine, cut into 1-inch (2.5 cm) strips	500 g
1/4 tsp	garlic powder	1 mL
1/4 tsp	lemon pepper	1 mL
1/4 tsp	salt	1 mL
Broth		
1 tbsp	olive oil	15 mL
1	small onion, chopped	1
2	cloves garlic, minced	2
2 1/2 cups	beef broth (store-bought or see recipe, page 126)	625 mL
1	can (14 oz/398 mL) crushed tomatoes, with juice	1
4 tsp	tomato paste	20 mL
1/2 tsp	dried oregano	2 mL
1/2 tsp	dried basil	2 mL
1/4 cup	freshly grated Parmesan cheese (preferably Parmigiano-Reggiano)	50 mL

1. Season veal strips with garlic powder, lemon pepper and salt. Roll strips and refrigerate, covered, for at least 1 hour.

2. In a large saucepan, heat oil over medium heat. Add onion and garlic; sauté until softened. Add beef broth, crushed tomatoes, tomato paste, oregano and basil. Bring to a boil. Reduce heat and simmer for 20 minutes. Immediately transfer to fondue pot, setting flame to keep at a simmer.

3. Spear veal roll with fondue fork. Fondue for 5 to 6 minutes or until cooked through and no longer pink. Dip veal in freshly grated Parmesan.

Italian Wedding Broth with Veal

1 lb	veal scaloppine, cut into 1-inch (2.5 cm) strips	500 g

Broth

5 cups	chicken broth (store-bought or see recipe, page 127)	1.25 L
2	cloves garlic, minced	2
2 tbsp	chopped fresh parsley (or 2 tsp/10 mL dried)	25 mL
1 tbsp	chopped fresh basil (or 1 tsp/5 mL dried)	15 mL
2 tsp	dried Italian seasoning	10 mL
2 cups	chopped spinach	500 mL

1. Roll up strips of veal and place on a large serving platter. Cover and set aside.

2. *Broth:* In a large saucepan, combine chicken broth, garlic, parsley, basil and Italian seasoning. Bring to a boil. Reduce heat and simmer, covered, for 10 minutes. Add spinach and simmer for 5 minutes. Immediately transfer to fondue pot, setting flame to keep at a simmer.

3. Spear veal roll with fondue fork. Fondue for 3 to 5 minutes or until cooked to desired doneness.

Serves 4

Tips
You can use beef tenderloin in place of veal.

When you are finished cooking the meat, you can add cooked pasta, such as shells or other small pasta, to the broth to create a wonderful soup.

Make ahead
Broth can be prepared in advance and then boiled on the stovetop prior to transferring to fondue pot.

Serve with...
Red pepper aioli, gremolata, honey mustard.

Veal and Wild Mushroom Fondue

Tip

Kosher salt, also known as coarse salt, is a great flavor infuser. Its coarse crystals can also be used for texture in some dishes and less is required than regular table salt, or sodium chloride.

Make ahead

Prepare marinade in advance and marinate chicken breast pieces for several hours before the fondue meal.

Serve with...

Zesty mayonnaise, sweet mustard dip, plum sauce.

Marinade

3 tbsp	dried wild or exotic mushrooms, soaked in boiling water for 15 minutes, then drained	45 mL
2	cloves garlic, minced	2
1 tbsp	olive oil	15 mL
1 tbsp	water	15 mL
2 tsp	balsamic vinegar	10 mL
¼ tsp	dried rosemary	1 mL
¼ tsp	dried thyme	1 mL
¼ tsp	kosher salt	1 mL
	Freshly ground black pepper to taste	
1 lb	veal scaloppine, cut into 1-inch (2.5 cm) strips	500 g

Broth

5 cups	beef broth (store-bought or see recipe, page 126)	1.25 L
1 cup	canned crushed tomatoes	250 mL
½ cup	red wine	125 mL
1 tsp	chili garlic paste	5 mL
1 tsp	granulated sugar	5 mL

1. *Marinade:* In a food processor, combine mushrooms, garlic, oil, water, vinegar, rosemary, thyme, salt and pepper; process to form a paste.

2. In a shallow casserole, brush veal strips with marinade, making sure that all pieces are well coated. Cover and refrigerate for at least 1 hour.

3. *Broth:* In a large saucepan, combine beef broth, tomatoes, wine, chili garlic paste and sugar. Bring to a boil. Reduce heat and simmer, covered, for 15 minutes. Immediately transfer to fondue pot, setting flame to keep at a simmer.

4. Remove veal strip from marinade, roll and spear with fondue fork. Fondue for 3 to 5 minutes or until cooked to desired doneness.

Saucy Beef or Pork Fondue

Marinade

½ tsp	dry mustard	2 mL
¼ tsp	ground cinnamon	1 mL
Pinch	ground allspice	Pinch
Pinch	ground cloves	Pinch
¼ cup	cider vinegar	50 mL
¼ cup	plum jam	50 mL
¼ cup	water	50 mL
	Salt and freshly ground black pepper to taste	
1 lb	beef or pork tenderloin, thinly sliced and cut into 1-inch (2.5 cm) strips	500 g

Broth

5 cups	beef broth (store-bought or see recipe, page 126)	1.25 L

1. **Marinade:** In a saucepan over medium heat, whisk together mustard, cinnamon, allspice, cloves, vinegar, jam, water, salt and pepper. Bring to a boil, whisking constantly. Remove from heat and set aside.

2. In a shallow casserole, brush beef or pork strips with marinade, making sure that all pieces are well coated. Cover and refrigerate for at least 1 hour.

3. **Broth:** In a large saucepan over high heat, bring beef broth to a boil. Immediately transfer to fondue pot, setting flame to keep at a simmer.

4. Remove beef or pork strip from marinade, roll and spear with fondue fork. Fondue for 3 to 5 minutes or until cooked to desired doneness.

Serves 4

This flavorful fondue appeals to children and adults alike.

Tip
Pair it with Classic Swiss Cheese Fondue (see recipe, page 28).

Make ahead
Prepare marinade in advance and marinate beef or pork tenderloin pieces for several hours before the fondue meal.

Serve with...
Plum sauce, sweet mustard dip, Japanese soy sauce, horseradish dip.

Apricot-Glazed Pork Tenderloin

Tips

You may replace the canned apricots with jarred puréed apricots (baby food); combine ingredients by hand rather than in a blender.

Use canned beef broth in place of the onion broth.

Make ahead

Prepare marinade in advance and marinate pork for several hours before the fondue meal.

Serve with...

Tzatziki, honey mustard, lemon sauce.

Marinade

½ cup	drained canned apricots	125 mL
1 tbsp	packed brown sugar	15 mL
1 tbsp	ketchup	15 mL
2 tsp	freshly squeezed lemon juice	10 mL
1 tsp	Dijon mustard	5 mL
½ tsp	hot pepper sauce (optional)	2 mL
¼ tsp	ground ginger	1 mL
¼ tsp	garlic powder	1 mL
	Salt and freshly ground black pepper to taste	
1 lb	pork tenderloin, thinly sliced and cut into 1-inch (2.5 cm) strips	500 g

Broth

5 cups	Quick Onion Broth (see recipe, page 137)	1.25 L

1. *Marinade:* In a blender or food processor, purée apricots. Add brown sugar, ketchup, lemon juice, mustard, hot pepper sauce (if using), ginger, garlic powder, salt and pepper. Blend or process until smooth.

2. In a shallow casserole, cover pork strips with marinade, tossing to coat well. Cover and refrigerate for at least 1 hour.

3. *Broth:* In a large saucepan, bring broth to a boil. Immediately transfer to fondue pot, setting flame to keep at a simmer.

4. Remove pork strip from marinade, roll and spear with fondue fork. Fondue for 3 to 5 minutes or until cooked to desired doneness.

Orange Pork Tenderloin Fondue

Marinade

1 cup	fresh orange juice	250 mL
1 tbsp	dried onion flakes	15 mL
2 tsp	packed brown sugar	10 mL
1 tsp	finely grated orange zest	5 mL
½ tsp	dried oregano	2 mL
¼ tsp	dried thyme	1 mL
	Salt and freshly ground black pepper to taste	
1 lb	pork tenderloin, thinly sliced and cut into 1-inch (2.5 cm) strips	500 g

Broth

5 cups	beef broth (store-bought or see recipe, page 126)	1.25 L

1. *Marinade:* In a bowl, combine orange juice, onion flakes, brown sugar, orange zest, oregano, thyme, salt and pepper; mix well.

2. In a shallow casserole, cover veal strips with marinade, tossing to coat well. Cover and refrigerate for at least 1 hour.

3. *Broth:* In a large saucepan, bring beef broth to a boil. Immediately transfer to fondue pot, setting flame to keep at a simmer.

4. Remove veal strip from marinade, roll and spear with fondue fork. Fondue for 3 to 5 minutes or until cooked to desired doneness.

Tip

A zester is ideally suited to removing the flavorful zest from the rind of an orange or lemon, without including the bitter white pith underneath. If you don't have a zester, you can use a fine grater, but be sure to grate just the surface.

Make ahead

Prepare marinade in advance and marinate pork tenderloin for several hours before the fondue meal.

Serve with...

Mint yogurt dip, sweet mustard dip, lemon sauce.

Thai Pork Fondue in Lemon Grass Broth

Tip

Depending on the size of the limes, you will need 2 or 3 limes to get ¼ cup (50 mL) lime juice.

To prepare lemon grass, peel outer coating of stem leaving only lower 2½ inches (6 cm), the most tender part. Cut off about 1 inch (2.5 cm) from bottom of bulb and then use remaining white part for mincing. If you can't find lemon grass, substitute 2 strips lemon zest for each stalk.

Make ahead

Prepare marinade in advance and marinate pork tenderloin pieces for several hours before the fondue meal.

Serve with...

Thai peanut sauce, chili garlic sauce, sweet Thai dip.

Marinade

¼ cup	freshly squeezed lime juice	50 mL
2 tbsp	cold water	25 mL
2 tbsp	vegetable oil	25 mL
2	cloves garlic, minced	2
1 tsp	ground coriander	5 mL
Pinch	cayenne pepper	Pinch
	Salt and freshly ground black pepper to taste	
1 lb	pork tenderloin, thinly sliced and cut into 1-inch (2.5 cm) strips	500 g

Broth

2 tsp	vegetable oil	10 mL
2	shallots, minced	2
5 cups	beef broth (store-bought or see recipe, page 126)	1.25 L
2 tbsp	chopped fresh cilantro	25 mL
2 tbsp	chopped fresh mint	25 mL
2	stalks lemon grass, minced	2
1 tsp	fish sauce	5 mL
Pinch	hot pepper flakes	Pinch

1. *Marinade:* In a bowl, combine lime juice, water, oil, garlic, coriander, cayenne, salt and black pepper; mix well.

2. In a shallow casserole, cover pork strips with marinade, tossing to coat well. Cover and refrigerate for at least 1 hour.

3. *Broth:* In a large saucepan, heat oil over medium heat. Add shallots and sauté until softened. Add beef broth, cilantro, mint, lemon grass, fish sauce and hot pepper flakes. Bring to a boil. Reduce heat and simmer for 20 minutes. Immediately transfer to fondue pot, setting flame to keep at a simmer.

4. Remove pork from marinade, roll and spear with fondue fork. Fondue for 3 to 5 minutes or until cooked to desired doneness.

Greek Lamb Fondue

Marinade

¼ cup	freshly squeezed lemon juice	50 mL
2	cloves garlic, minced	2
1 tbsp	olive oil	15 mL
1 tsp	dried oregano	5 mL
½ tsp	salt	2 mL
1 lb	loin or leg of lamb, cut into 1-inch (2.5 cm) cubes	500 g

Broth

5 cups	beef broth (store-bought or see recipe, page 126)	1.25 L

1. *Marinade:* In a bowl, combine lemon juice, garlic, oil, oregano and salt; mix well.

2. In a shallow casserole, cover lamb cubes with marinade, tossing to coat well. Cover and refrigerate for at least 1 hour.

3. *Broth:* In a large saucepan, bring beef broth to a boil. Immediately transfer to fondue pot, setting flame to keep at a simmer.

4. Remove lamb from marinade and spear with fondue fork. Fondue for 3 to 5 minutes or until cooked to desired doneness.

Serves 4

For a Greek-themed meal, serve with Greek Feta and Mint Fondue (see recipe, page 68), accompanied by Greek salad, lemon potatoes and pita bread.

Tip
Loin of lamb is the most tender cut of lamb and recommended for fondues. If you opt to use a less expensive cut, be sure to marinate it for longer so it won't be as tough. Cubed leg of lamb is one alternative.

Make ahead
Prepare your marinade earlier in the day and marinate lamb cubes for several hours. At fondue time, simply boil beef broth on stovetop and transfer to fondue pot.

Serve with...
Mint yogurt dip, garlic aïoli, sweet mustard dip, lemon dill dip.

Mediterranean Pomegranate Fondue with Spiced Broth

Tip

Serve with couscous as a side dish.

Make ahead

Prepare marinade in advance and marinate lamb for several hours before the fondue meal.

Marinade

¼ cup	pomegranate juice	50 mL
2 tbsp	liquid honey	25 mL
2 tbsp	water	25 mL
	Salt and freshly ground black pepper to taste	
1 lb	loin or leg of lamb, cut into 1-inch (2.5 cm) cubes	500 g

Broth

2 tsp	olive oil	10 mL
1	onion, chopped	1
1	jalapeño pepper, seeded and minced	1
2	cloves garlic, minced	2
1	piece (1 inch/2.5 cm) gingerroot, minced	1
5 cups	chicken broth (store-bought or see recipe, page 127)	1.25 L
1	can (28 oz/796 mL) diced tomatoes, with juice	1
1	cinnamon stick (about 2 inches/5 cm)	1
½ cup	chopped fresh parsley	125 mL
1 tsp	ground turmeric	5 mL
Pinch	crumbled saffron	Pinch
Pinch	cayenne pepper	Pinch

1. *Marinade:* In a bowl, whisk together pomegranate juice, honey, water, salt and black pepper.

2. In a shallow casserole, cover lamb cubes with marinade, tossing to coat well. Cover and refrigerate for at least 1 hour.

3. *Broth:* In a large saucepan, heat oil over medium heat. Add onion, jalapeño, garlic and ginger; sauté until softened. Add chicken broth, tomatoes, with juice, cinnamon stick, parsley, turmeric, saffron and cayenne. Bring to a boil. Reduce heat and simmer, covered, for 30 minutes. If too thick, add up to $1/2$ cup (125 mL) boiling water. Transfer to fondue pot, setting flame to keep at a simmer.

4. Remove lamb cube from marinade and spear with fondue fork. Fondue for 2 to 4 minutes or until cooked to desired doneness.

Serve with...
Tzatziki, hummus, cilantro coulis.

Middle Eastern Lamb Fondue

Serves 4

The combination of spices in this dish is impressive, and the depth of flavor makes it the perfect centerpiece for a fondue party.

Tip
Serve with couscous as a side dish.

Make ahead
Prepare marinade in advance and marinate lamb for several hours before the fondue meal.

Serve with...
Tzatziki, hummus, hot pepper sauce, cilantro coulis.

Marinade

1 tbsp	olive oil	15 mL
1 tbsp	water	15 mL
1 tbsp	freshly squeezed lemon juice	15 mL
1	clove garlic, finely minced	1
1	shallot, finely minced	1
1 tsp	ground coriander	5 mL
1 tsp	ground cumin	5 mL
½ tsp	ground cardamom	2 mL
½ tsp	dried parsley	2 mL
¼ tsp	dried mint	1 mL
	Salt and freshly ground black pepper to taste	
1 lb	loin or leg of lamb, cut into 1-inch (2.5 cm) cubes	500 g

Broth

5 cups	beef broth (store-bought or see recipe, page 126)	1.25 L

1. *Marinade:* In a bowl, whisk together olive oil, water, lemon juice, garlic, shallot, coriander, cumin, cardamom, parsley, mint, salt and pepper.

2. In a shallow casserole, cover lamb cubes with marinade, tossing to coat well. Cover and refrigerate for at least 1 hour.

3. *Broth:* In a large saucepan, bring beef broth to a boil. Immediately transfer to fondue pot, setting flame to keep at a simmer.

4. Remove lamb cube from marinade and spear with fondue fork. Fondue for 2 to 4 minutes or until cooked to desired doneness.

Moroccan Fondue

1 lb	loin or leg of lamb, thinly sliced and cut into 1-inch (2.5 cm) strips	500 g
Broth		
5 cups	chicken broth (store-bought or see recipe, page 127)	1.25 L
½ cup	chopped fresh parsley	125 mL
1 tsp	ground ginger	5 mL
1 tsp	ground turmeric	5 mL
½ tsp	ground cinnamon	2 mL
¼ tsp	ground nutmeg	1 mL
¼ tsp	freshly ground black pepper	1 mL

1. Roll up strips of lamb and place on a large serving platter. Cover and set aside.

2. *Broth:* In a large saucepan, combine chicken broth, parsley, ginger, turmeric, cinnamon, nutmeg and pepper. Bring to a boil. Reduce heat and simmer, covered, for 15 minutes. Immediately transfer to fondue pot, setting flame to keep at a simmer.

3. Spear lamb roll with fondue fork. Fondue for about 3 minutes or until cooked to desired doneness.

Serves 4

Tips

For a little extra zing to the broth, add ½ tsp (2 mL) hot pepper flakes.

Beef tenderloin or boneless skinless chicken breast can replace lamb.

Make ahead

Slice lamb, set on platter and refrigerate.

Prepare broth in advance. When ready to use, bring to a boil and transfer to fondue pot.

Serve with...

Mint yogurt dip, roasted red pepper dip, salsa verde.

Mongolian Hot Pot

This recipe is perfect for entertaining — a very satisfying main course, followed by a divine soup.

Tips

Mongolian Hot Pot Dipping Sauce (see recipe, page 255) is a must for this fondue.

Prepare rice stick noodles just before they will be used. To prepare rice stick noodles, simply soak in warm water for 10 minutes. Cut with kitchen shears if desired before adding to fondue pot.

1½ lbs	loin or leg of lamb, thinly sliced and cut into 1-inch (2.5 cm) strips	750 g
Vegetable platter		
4 oz	spinach leaves, cut into strips	125 g
8 oz	bok choy, cut into strips	250 g
2	red and/or green bell peppers, cut into large chunks	2
1 cup	sliced mushrooms	250 mL
½ cup	bean sprouts	125 mL
2	green onions, chopped	2
Broth		
6 cups	beef broth (store-bought or see recipe, page 126)	1.5 L
1	shallot, minced	1
2	cloves garlic, minced	2
2 tsp	grated gingerroot	10 mL
	Mongolian Hot Pot Dipping Sauce (see recipe, page 255)	
2 tbsp	chopped fresh cilantro	25 mL
4 oz	rice stick or bean thread noodles, cooked	125 g
	Chopped fresh cilantro for garnish	
	Hot pepper flakes for garnish	

1. Roll up strips of lamb and place on a large serving platter. Cover and set aside.

2. *Vegetable platter:* On another large platter, decoratively arrange spinach, bok choy, peppers, mushrooms, bean sprouts and green onions.

3. *Broth:* In a large saucepan, combine beef broth, shallot, garlic and ginger. Bring to a boil. Simmer, covered, for 15 minutes. Immediately transfer to fondue pot, setting flame to keep at a simmer.

4. Provide each guest with a bowl of Mongolian Hot Pot Dipping Sauce. Spear a lamb roll with fondue fork and fondue for about 3 minutes or until cooked to desired doneness. Dip cooked lamb in sauce before eating. Spear mushrooms and peppers and fondue in similar fashion.

5. When all of the meat has been eaten, it's time for the soup. Add spinach, bok choy, bean sprouts and any remaining mushrooms and peppers to fondue pot. Add the 2 tbsp (25 mL) cilantro and noodles and simmer for about 3 minutes. Ladle into individual bowls. Garnish with additional dipping sauce, cilantro and hot pepper flakes.

Make ahead

Prepare the Mongolian Hot Pot Dipping sauce.

Slice the lamb and refrigerate until needed.

Cut up the vegetables and set on a platter.

Prepare the broth earlier in the day. Before the fondue, simply boil on the stovetop as directed and transfer to fondue pot.

Serve with...

Mongolian Hot Pot Dipping Sauce, chili garlic sauce, tomato curry sauce, Thai peanut sauce.

Butter Chicken Fondue

Serves 4

Tips

Do not use fat-free yogurt for this recipe — 2% works best, as it is thicker.

To turn this fondue into a meal, serve with a vegetable platter consisting of mushrooms, sliced bell peppers and broccoli florets. Fondue vegetables to desired doneness. When about one-quarter of the chicken remains, add it and any remaining vegetables to fondue pot. Simmer for several minutes, then add soaked and drained rice stick noodles. Serve as a soup to end the meal.

Marinade

⅔ cup	plain 2% yogurt	150 mL
1 tsp	garam masala	5 mL
½ tsp	ground coriander	2 mL
¼ tsp	cayenne pepper	1 mL
¼ tsp	ground cinnamon	1 mL
Pinch	ground cloves	Pinch
Pinch	ground cardamom	Pinch
1 lb	boneless skinless chicken thighs, cut into 1-inch (2.5 cm) cubes	500 g

Broth

1 tbsp	butter	5 mL
1	onion, minced	1
2	cloves garlic, minced	2
1	piece (1 inch/2.5 cm) gingerroot, minced	1
5 cups	chicken broth (store-bought or see recipe, page 127)	1.25 L
1	can (14 oz/398 mL) diced tomatoes, with juice	1
1	bay leaf	1

1. *Marinade:* In a bowl, combine yogurt, garam masala, coriander, cayenne, cinnamon, cloves and cardamom. Mix well.

2. In a shallow casserole, cover chicken cubes with marinade, tossing to coat well. Cover and refrigerate for at least 1 hour.

3. *Broth:* In a large saucepan, melt butter over medium heat. Add onion, garlic and ginger; sauté until softened. Add chicken broth, tomatoes, with juice, and bay leaf. Bring to a boil. Reduce heat and simmer, covered, for 20 minutes. Immediately transfer to fondue pot, setting flame to keep at a simmer.

4. Remove chicken cube from marinade and spear with fondue fork. Fondue for 2 to 4 minutes or until cooked through.

A fondue party offers the ideal occasion to design a themed menu around ethnic culinary traditions. From Mexican to Middle Eastern, from Italian to Greek, you'll find a range of recipes in each chapter of *The Fondue Bible* that will allow you to create a terrific themed fondue party. Serve an Indian-themed meal starring this recipe, and start with Curry Cheese Fondue (page 45) or Quick Curry, Cheese and Mushroom Fondue (page 46).

Make ahead

Prepare marinade in advance and marinate chicken for several hours before the fondue meal.

Broth can be prepared in advance and then boiled on the stovetop prior to transferring to fondue pot.

Serve with...

Tomato curry sauce, cilantro coulis, spicy sesame mayonnaise.

Black Sesame Seed Chicken Fondue

Tip

Used in Asian and Middle Eastern cooking, black sesame seeds impart not only a unique appearance but also a distinctive flavor. You can find them in specialty stores.

Make ahead

Complete to the end of Step 2. Refrigerate until needed.

Serve with...

Asian dipping sauce, Thai peanut sauce, cilantro coulis.

Marinade

3 tbsp	water	45 mL
1 tbsp	olive oil	15 mL
1	clove garlic, finely minced	1
	Juice of ½ lemon	
	Salt and freshly ground black pepper to taste	
1 lb	boneless skinless chicken breasts, thinly sliced and cut into 1-inch (2.5 cm) strips	500 g
½ cup	black sesame seeds	125 mL

Broth

5 cups	chicken broth (store-bought or see recipe, page 127)	1.25 L

1. *Marinade:* In a bowl, whisk together water, olive oil, garlic, lemon juice, salt and pepper.

2. In a shallow casserole, cover chicken strips with marinade, tossing to coat well. Roll chicken strips one at a time in black sesame seeds, coating well. Roll up chicken strips and place on a large serving platter. Cover and refrigerate for at least 1 hour.

3. *Broth:* In a large saucepan, bring chicken broth to a boil. Immediately transfer to fondue pot, setting flame to keep at a simmer.

4. Spear chicken roll with fondue fork. Fondue for 2 to 4 minutes or until cooked through.

Chicken Broth and Shallots with Spicy Chicken or Pork

Dry rub

1 tsp	dry mustard	5 mL
1 tsp	paprika	5 mL
½ tsp	cayenne pepper	2 mL
½ tsp	ground cumin	2 mL
¼ tsp	garlic powder	1 mL
	Salt and freshly ground black pepper to taste	
1 lb	boneless skinless chicken breasts or pork tenderloin, thinly sliced and cut into 1-inch (2.5 cm) strips	500 g

Broth

1 tbsp	olive oil	15 mL
2	shallots, minced	2
5 cups	chicken broth (store-bought or see recipe, page 127)	1.25 L
2 tbsp	chopped fresh parsley	25 mL

1. *Dry rub:* In a bowl, combine mustard, paprika, cayenne, cumin, salt and black pepper; mix well.

2. Place pieces of chicken or pork one at a time in dry rub, turning to coat well. Transfer coated pieces to platter. Cover and refrigerate for at least 1 hour.

3. *Broth:* In a large saucepan, heat oil over medium heat. Add shallots and sauté for 3 to 5 minutes or until softened (but not browned). Add chicken broth; bring to a boil. Immediately transfer to fondue pot, setting flame to keep at a simmer. Add parsley.

4. Spear chicken or pork with fondue fork. Fondue for 3 to 5 minutes or until cooked through.

Serves 4

Tip
Because the broth absorbs spices from the marinated meat cooked in it, you end up with a very flavorful base for soup. Add rice stick noodles once most of the meat has been fondued.

Make ahead
Combine marinade ingredients and marinate chicken or pork for several hours before the fondue.

Prepare broth in advance.

Serve with...
Blue cheese dip, plum sauce, Dijonnaise, tomato curry sauce, roasted red pepper dip.

Chicken-in-a-Hurry Fondue

Don't be fooled by the long ingredient list — this really is a quick fondue! The marinade is a tasty concoction of many spices and condiments that most of us have on hand.

Make ahead

This fondue is great for easy entertaining. Prepare marinade in advance and marinate chicken for several hours.

Serve with...

Plum sauce, soy sauce, sweet and sour sauce, Dijonnaise.

Marinade

¼ cup	ketchup	50 mL
2 tbsp	soy sauce	25 mL
1 tbsp	cider vinegar	15 mL
2 tsp	packed brown sugar	10 mL
2 tsp	dried onion flakes	10 mL
½ tsp	curry powder	2 mL
½ tsp	dry mustard	2 mL
½ tsp	garlic powder	2 mL
½ tsp	salt	2 mL
¼ tsp	freshly ground black pepper	1 mL
1 lb	boneless skinless chicken breasts, thinly sliced and cut into 1-inch (2.5 cm) strips	500 g

Broth

2	cans (each 10 oz/284 mL) chicken broth, diluted with 2 cans water	2

1. *Marinade:* In a bowl, combine ketchup, soy sauce, vinegar, brown sugar, onion flakes, curry powder, mustard, garlic powder, salt and pepper; mix well.

2. In a shallow casserole, cover chicken pieces with marinade, tossing to coat well. Cover and refrigerate for at least 1 hour.

3. *Broth:* In a large saucepan, bring chicken broth to a boil. Immediately transfer to fondue pot, setting flame to keep at a simmer.

4. Remove chicken from marinade and spear with fondue fork. Fondue for 3 to 5 minutes or until cooked through.

Honey Garlic Chicken Fondue

Marinade

½ cup	liquid honey	125 mL
⅓ cup	soy sauce	75 mL
4	cloves garlic, minced	4
1 lb	boneless skinless chicken breasts, thinly sliced and cut into 1-inch (2.5 cm) strips	500 g

Broth

5 cups	chicken broth (store-bought or see recipe, page 127)	1.25 L

1. *Marinade:* In a saucepan over medium heat, stir together honey, soy sauce and garlic. Remove from heat and allow to cool slightly.

2. In a shallow casserole, cover chicken with marinade, making sure that all pieces are well coated. Cover and refrigerate for at least 1 hour.

3. *Broth:* In a large saucepan, bring chicken broth to a boil. Immediately transfer to fondue pot, setting flame to keep at a simmer.

4. Remove chicken from marinade and spear with fondue fork. Fondue for 2 to 4 minutes or until cooked through.

Tip
If you are serving several main fondues (it's always nice to offer guests a choice) and you wind up with leftover raw chicken, you can fondue the remaining pieces in the broth to make a tasty soup that you can enjoy the next day — just add cooked noodles. You can also stir-fry leftover chicken and use it the next day to make fajitas.

Make ahead
Prepare marinade early in the day and marinate chicken for several hours in advance of the fondue meal.

Serve with...
Chili vinegar, blue cheese dip, Dijonnaise, zesty mayonnaise.

Hungarian Chicken Paprika

Marinade

½ cup	sour cream	125 mL
2 tsp	Hungarian paprika	10 mL
½ tsp	cayenne pepper	2 mL
	Salt and freshly ground green peppercorns to taste	
1 lb	boneless skinless chicken breasts, cut into 1-inch (2.5 cm) cubes	500 g

Broth

1 tbsp	vegetable oil	5 mL
1	onion, minced	1
2	cloves garlic, minced	2
½	green bell pepper, chopped	½
5 cups	chicken broth (store-bought or see recipe, page 127)	1.25 L

1. *Marinade:* In a bowl, combine sour cream, paprika, cayenne, salt and green pepper. Mix well.

2. In a shallow casserole, cover chicken cubes with marinade, tossing to coat well. Cover and refrigerate for at least 1 hour.

3. *Broth:* In a large saucepan, heat oil over medium heat. Add onion, garlic and green pepper; sauté until softened. Add chicken broth and bring to a boil. Reduce heat and simmer, covered, for 15 minutes. Immediately transfer to fondue pot, setting flame to keep at a simmer.

4. Remove chicken cube from marinade and spear with fondue fork. Fondue for 2 to 4 minutes or until cooked through.

Tips

You can use boneless skinless chicken thighs in place of chicken breasts.

Use light sour cream to lighten up the dish.

This marinated chicken also works very well fondued in oil.

To turn this fondue into a meal, serve with a vegetable platter consisting of mushrooms, sliced red bell peppers and broccoli florets. Fondue vegetables to desired doneness. When about one-quarter of the chicken remains, add it and any remaining vegetables to fondue pot. Simmer for several minutes, then add boiled egg noodles. Serve as a soup to end the meal.

Make ahead

Broth can be prepared in advance and then boiled on stovetop prior to transferring to fondue pot.

Serve with...

Dijonnaise, sweet-and-sour sauce, honey mustard.

Indian Mango Broth with Chicken

Broth

1 tbsp	vegetable oil	15 mL
1	shallot, minced	1
5 cups	chicken broth (store-bought or see recipe, page 127)	1.25 L
1 tbsp	minced gingerroot	15 mL
½ tsp	curry powder	2 mL
½ tsp	ground turmeric	2 mL
¼ tsp	cayenne pepper	1 mL
¼ tsp	ground cumin	1 mL
½ cup	chopped mango (about ½ mango)	125 mL
1 lb	boneless skinless chicken breasts, thinly sliced and cut into 1-inch (2.5 cm) strips	500 g

1. *Broth:* In a large saucepan, heat oil over medium heat. Add shallot and sauté for 2 minutes or until softened. Add chicken broth, ginger, curry powder, turmeric, cayenne pepper and cumin; simmer, covered, for 15 minutes to allow flavors to blend.

2. Add mango to broth and simmer, uncovered, for another 5 minutes. Transfer broth to fondue pot, setting flame to keep at a simmer.

3. Spear chicken with fondue fork and fondue for 2 to 4 minutes or until cooked through.

Tips

This recipe also works well with boneless turkey breast in place of the chicken.

To turn this fondue into a meal, serve with a vegetable platter consisting of bok choy cut into strips, green and red pepper chunks, mushroom halves, and cauliflower and broccoli florets. Fondue chicken and vegetables to desired doneness. When about one-quarter of chicken remains, add it to fondue pot. Simmer for several minutes, then add noodles of your choice (soaked or precooked). Serve as soup to end the meal.

Make ahead

Prepare broth up to the end of Step 1. At mealtime, bring broth to a boil. Reduce heat to simmer, add mango and simmer as directed for another 5 minutes.

Serve with...

Thai peanut sauce, red curry paste, mango salsa or chutney.

Hot-and-Sour Broth
with Chicken

This broth also works well with shrimp, tofu cubes and pieces of pork tenderloin.

Tips

If you prefer your broth a little less spicy, reduce chili garlic sauce by half. To make it extra sour, add 1 tbsp (15 mL) lemon juice.

Never place raw chicken on the same platter as vegetables. Ensure guests do not place raw chicken on their dinner plate. Equip each guest with a separate bowl in which to place the raw chicken and from which they can spear it onto the fondue fork.

Broth

5 cups	chicken broth (store-bought or see recipe, page 127)	1.25 L
1½ tsp	minced gingerroot	7 mL
4	dried Chinese mushrooms, soaked in boiling water for 15 minutes, then drained and chopped	4
2 tsp	cornstarch	10 mL
2 tbsp	water	25 mL
	Salt and freshly ground black pepper to taste	
2 tbsp	cider vinegar	25 mL
2 tbsp	freshly squeezed lemon juice	25 mL
1 tbsp	sesame oil	15 mL
1 tbsp	chili garlic sauce	15 mL
2	green onions, chopped	2

Vegetable platter

1	can (8 oz/227 mL) bamboo shoots, drained	1
2 cups	bean sprouts	500 mL
2 cups	fresh halved mushrooms	500 mL
1 lb	boneless skinless chicken breasts, thinly sliced and cut into 1-inch (2.5 cm) strips	500 g
4 oz	rice vermicelli noodles, soaked in hot water for 15 minutes and drained	125 g

1. *Broth:* In a large saucepan over medium-high heat, bring chicken broth to a boil. Add ginger and rehydrated mushrooms. Whisk together cornstarch and water until dissolved; stir into broth. Season to taste with salt and pepper. Add vinegar, lemon juice, sesame oil and chili garlic sauce. Reduce heat to medium-low and add green onions; simmer, covered, for 15 minutes to allow flavors to blend.

2. *Vegetable platter:* Meanwhile, assemble bamboo shoots, bean sprouts and mushrooms on a platter. Place raw chicken on a separate platter. Transfer broth to fondue pot, setting flame to keep at a simmer.

3. Spear a piece of chicken with fondue fork and fondue for 2 to 4 minutes. Vegetables can also be fondued in broth.

4. When one-quarter of the chicken is left, add to fondue pot and simmer for several minutes. Add vermicelli noodles, along with remaining bamboo shoots, bean sprouts and mushrooms. Serve as soup to end the meal.

Make ahead

Prepare vegetable platter and slice up chicken breasts.

Prepare hot-and-sour broth earlier in the day. Bring to a boil on stovetop and transfer to fondue pot.

Serve with...

Plum sauce, Asian dipping sauce, sweet-and-sour sauce, wasabi mayonnaise.

Lemon Chicken Fondue

This fondue offers a double dose of lemon — from the lemon marinade and the lemon-infused broth.

Tip

If fresh oregano is not available, replace with one-third the quantity of dried. For example, to replace 1¹/₂ tsp (7 mL) fresh oregano, use ¹/₂ tsp (2 mL) dried.

Make ahead

Prepare marinade early in day and leave chicken to marinate for several hours in advance of fondue.

Prepare broth up to the end of Step 3. At meal time, quickly bring broth to a boil and then transfer to fondue pot.

Serve with...

Mint yogurt dip, salsa verde, garlic aïoli.

Marinade

¹/₄ cup	freshly squeezed lemon juice	50 mL
1 tbsp	olive oil	15 mL
1 tbsp	water (approx.)	15 mL
1¹/₂ tsp	chopped fresh oregano	7 mL
¹/₂ tsp	garlic powder	2 mL
¹/₂ tsp	lemon pepper	2 mL
¹/₄ tsp	salt	1 mL
1 lb	boneless skinless chicken breasts, thinly sliced and cut into 1-inch (2.5 cm) strips	500 g

Broth

1 tbsp	olive oil	15 mL
2	cloves garlic, minced	2
5 cups	chicken broth (store-bought or see recipe, page 127)	1.25 L
¹/₄ cup	dry white wine	50 mL
2 tbsp	freshly squeezed lemon juice	25 mL
1 tbsp	chopped fresh oregano	15 mL
2 tsp	finely grated lemon zest	10 mL
	Salt and black pepper to taste	

1. *Marinade:* In a bowl, combine lemon juice, oil, water, oregano, garlic powder, lemon pepper and salt; mix well. Add more water, if necessary, for a pourable consistency.

2. In a shallow casserole, cover chicken pieces with marinade, tossing to coat well. Cover and refrigerate for at least 1 hour.

3. *Broth:* In a large saucepan, heat oil over medium heat. Add garlic and sauté for 2 minutes or until softened (but not browned). Add chicken broth, wine, lemon juice, oregano, lemon zest, salt and black pepper; bring to a boil. Reduce heat and simmer for 15 minutes to allow flavors to blend. Transfer to fondue pot, setting flame to keep at a simmer.

4. Remove chicken from marinade and spear with fondue fork. Fondue for 2 to 4 minutes or until cooked through.

Pesto Chicken Fondue

Marinade

2	cloves garlic	2
2 tbsp	sun-dried tomatoes	25 mL
2 tbsp	pine nuts, toasted (see tip, page 70)	25 mL
2 tbsp	chopped fresh basil	25 mL
1 tbsp	olive oil	15 mL
	Salt and freshly ground black pepper to taste	
1 lb	boneless skinless chicken breasts, thinly sliced and cut into 1-inch (2.5 cm) strips	500 g

Broth

5 cups	chicken broth (store-bought or see recipe, page 127)	1.25 L

1. *Marinade:* In a food processor, mince garlic. Add sun-dried tomatoes, pine nuts, basil, olive oil, salt and pepper; process to form a paste.

2. In a shallow casserole, brush chicken strips with marinade, making sure all pieces are well coated. Cover and refrigerate for at least 1 hour.

3. *Broth:* In a large saucepan, bring chicken broth to a boil. Immediately transfer to fondue pot, setting flame to keep at a simmer.

4. Remove chicken strip from marinade, roll and spear with fondue fork. Fondue for 2 to 4 minutes or until cooked through.

Serves 4

Tips

Sun-dried tomatoes packed in oil work best in this fondue. If using reconstituted sun-dried tomatoes, increase the olive oil by 1 tsp (5 mL).

You can also serve this chicken with Three-Herb Italian Broth Fondue (page 181).

To turn this fondue into a meal, serve with a vegetable platter consisting of mushrooms, sliced red and green bell peppers, zucchini slices and broccoli florets. Fondue vegetables to desired doneness. When about one-quarter of the chicken remains, add it and any remaining vegetables to fondue pot. Simmer for several minutes, then add cooked vermicelli or orzo. Serve as a soup to end the meal.

Make ahead

Broth can be prepared in advance and then boiled on the stovetop prior to transferring to fondue pot.

Serve with...

Gremolata, lemon dill dip, roasted red pepper dip.

Pineapple Chicken Fondue

Marinade

¼ cup	crushed canned pineapple, 1 cup (250 mL) juice reserved	50 mL
2	cloves garlic, minced	2
¼ cup	soy sauce	50 mL
2 tbsp	cider vinegar	25 mL
2 tsp	grated gingerroot	10 mL
1 lb	boneless skinless chicken breasts, thinly sliced and cut into 1-inch (2.5 cm) strips	500 g

Broth

5 cups	chicken broth (store-bought or see recipe, page 127)	1.25 L

1. *Marinade:* In a bowl, combine pineapple and reserved juice, garlic, soy sauce, vinegar and ginger; mix well.

2. In a shallow casserole, cover chicken pieces with marinade, tossing to coat well. Cover and refrigerate for at least 1 hour.

3. *Broth:* In a large saucepan, bring chicken broth to a boil. Immediately transfer to fondue pot, setting flame to keep at a simmer.

4. Remove chicken from marinade and spear with fondue fork. Fondue for 2 to 4 minutes or until cooked through.

Raspberry Chicken Fondue

Marinade

1/2 cup	frozen raspberries in syrup, thawed and puréed	125 mL
1/4 cup	olive oil	50 mL
1/4 cup	raspberry vinegar	50 mL
2	cloves garlic, minced	2
1 tsp	minced gingerroot	5 mL
	Salt and freshly ground black pepper to taste	
1 lb	boneless skinless chicken breasts, thinly sliced and cut into 1-inch (2.5 cm) strips	500 g

Broth

5 cups	chicken broth (store-bought or see recipe, page 127)	1.25 L

1. *Marinade:* In a bowl, combine raspberries, oil, raspberry vinegar, garlic, ginger, salt and pepper; mix well.

2. In a shallow casserole, cover chicken pieces with marinade, tossing to coat well. Cover and refrigerate for at least 1 hour.

3. *Broth:* In a large saucepan, bring chicken broth to a boil. Immediately transfer to fondue pot, setting flame to keep at a simmer.

4. Remove chicken from marinade and spear with fondue fork. Fondue for 2 to 4 minutes or until cooked through.

Serves 4

Tip
To give the marinade extra punch, add 1 tbsp (25 mL) Worcestershire sauce and 1/4 tsp (2 mL) paprika. To reduce tartness, stir 1 to 2 tsp (5 to 10 mL) sugar into marinade before brushing onto chicken.

Make ahead
Prepare marinade in advance and marinate chicken breast pieces for several hours before the fondue meal.

Serve with...
Asian dipping sauce, Thai peanut sauce, soy sauce.

Spicy Thai Fondue with Coconut Milk

Tips

You can use soy sauce in place of fish sauce, but the broth won't be quite as authentic.

If you prefer a less spicy broth, omit the Thai chili.

To turn this fondue into a meal, serve with a vegetable platter consisting of mushrooms, sliced bell peppers and broccoli florets. Fondue vegetables to desired doneness. When about one-quarter of the chicken remains, add it and any remaining vegetables to fondue pot. Simmer for several minutes, then add soaked and drained rice stick noodles. Serve as a soup to end the meal.

Make ahead

Broth can be prepared in advance and then boiled on the stovetop prior to transferring to fondue pot.

Serve with...

Sweet Thai dip, Thai peanut sauce, Asian dipping sauce.

1 lb	boneless skinless chicken breasts, thinly sliced and cut into 1-inch (2.5 cm) strips	500 g
Broth		
5 cups	chicken broth (store-bought or see recipe, page 127)	1.25 L
¾ cup	coconut milk	175 mL
2	cloves garlic, minced	2
2	green onions, minced	2
½	Thai chili pepper, seeded and minced	½
½ cup	chopped fresh cilantro	125 mL
1 tsp	grated lime zest	5 mL
2 tbsp	freshly squeezed lime juice	25 mL
2 tbsp	fish sauce (see tip, page 189)	25 mL
2 tbsp	minced fresh Thai basil	25 mL
1 tbsp	minced gingerroot	15 mL
1 tsp	granulated sugar	5 mL
1 tsp	Thai green curry paste	5 mL

1. Roll up strips of chicken and place on a large serving platter. Cover and refrigerate.

2. *Broth:* In a large saucepan, combine chicken broth, coconut milk, garlic, green onions, chili pepper, cilantro, lime zest, lime juice, fish sauce, basil, ginger, sugar and curry paste. Bring to a boil. Reduce heat and simmer, covered, for 15 minutes. Immediately transfer to fondue pot, setting flame to keep at a simmer.

3. Spear chicken roll with fondue fork. Fondue for 2 to 4 minutes or until cooked through.

Szechwan Sesame Chicken Fondue

Marinade

1½ tbsp	hoisin sauce	22 mL
1 tbsp	soy sauce	15 mL
1 tbsp	water	15 mL
2 tsp	liquid honey	10 mL
1	clove garlic, minced	1
1 tsp	minced gingerroot	5 mL
	Salt and freshly ground black pepper to taste	
1 tsp	sesame oil	5 mL
1 tsp	sesame seeds, toasted	5 mL
1 lb	boneless skinless chicken breasts, thinly sliced and cut into 1-inch (2.5 cm) strips	500 g

Broth

5 cups	chicken broth (store-bought or see recipe, page 127)	1.25 L

1. *Marinade:* In a saucepan over medium heat, combine hoisin sauce, soy sauce, water, honey, garlic, ginger, salt and pepper; stir until well mixed and honey is melted. Remove from heat; stir in sesame oil and sesame seeds.

2. In a shallow casserole, cover chicken with marinade, making sure that all pieces are well coated. Cover and refrigerate for at least 1 hour.

3. *Broth:* In a large saucepan, bring chicken broth to a boil. Immediately transfer to fondue pot, setting flame to keep at a simmer.

4. Remove chicken from marinade and spear with fondue fork. Fondue for 2 to 4 minutes or until cooked through.

Serves 4

Hoisin sauce, made from fermented soybeans, adds a unique flavor to the marinade in this recipe; there is really no substitute.

Tips

Toasting the sesame seeds adds extra flavor to the marinade. Just toast in a nonstick skillet over low heat for 3 to 5 minutes, turning once.

To give the broth a little extra punch, add 2 tbsp (25 mL) salsa verde.

Make ahead

Prepare marinade in advance and marinate chicken breast pieces for several hours before the fondue meal.

Serve with...

Sweet-and-sour sauce, sweet chili sauce, peanut sauce, soy sauce, salsa verde.

Wild Rice and Mushroom Broth with Hoisin-Marinated Chicken

The broth here gets its earthy flavor from both fresh and dried mushrooms. Serve it as a delicious soup at the end of the meal.

Tip

To turn this fondue into a meal, serve with a vegetable platter consisting of bok choy cut into strips, green and red pepper chunks, mushroom halves, and cauliflower and broccoli florets. Fondue chicken and vegetables to desired doneness. When about one-quarter of chicken remains, add it to fondue pot. Simmer for several minutes, then add noodles of your choice (soaked or precooked). Serve as soup to end the meal.

Marinade

¼ cup	hoisin sauce	50 mL
1½ tbsp	rice wine	22 mL
1	clove garlic, minced	1
1 tbsp	granulated sugar	15 mL
1 tbsp	minced gingerroot	15 mL
1 tbsp	sesame oil	15 mL
1 tbsp	soy sauce	15 mL
1 lb	boneless skinless chicken breasts, thinly sliced and cut into 1-inch (2.5 cm) strips	500 g

Broth

2 tsp	olive oil	10 mL
1	small onion, chopped	1
1	clove garlic, minced	1
¾ cup	chopped fresh mushrooms	175 mL
5 cups	chicken broth (store-bought or see recipe, page 127)	1.25 L
¼ cup	wild rice, rinsed	50 mL
2 tbsp	dried wild or exotic mushrooms (such as porcini), soaked in boiling water for 15 minutes, soaking liquid strained through cheesecloth and reserved	25 mL
	Salt and freshly ground black pepper to taste	
	Chopped fresh parsley for garnish	

1. *Marinade:* In a bowl, combine hoisin sauce, rice wine, garlic, sugar, ginger, sesame oil and soy sauce; mix well.

2. In a shallow casserole, cover chicken pieces with marinade, tossing to coat well. Cover and refrigerate for at least 1 hour.

3. *Broth:* In a large saucepan, heat oil over medium heat. Add onion, garlic and fresh mushrooms; sauté for 2 minutes or until softened. Add chicken broth, wild rice, rehydrated wild mushrooms and strained mushroom soaking liquid; bring to a boil. Reduce heat and simmer for 35 to 45 minutes or until rice is tender. Transfer to fondue pot, setting flame to keep at a simmer. Season with salt and pepper and garnish broth with parsley.

4. Remove chicken from marinade and spear with fondue fork. Fondue for 2 to 4 minutes or until cooked through.

Make ahead
Prepare marinade in advance and marinate chicken breast pieces for several hours before the fondue meal.

Serve with...
Horseradish dip, roasted red pepper dip, lemon sauce.

Thai Chicken Fondue

Tip

To turn this fondue into a meal, serve with a vegetable platter consisting of bok choy cut into strips, green and red pepper chunks, bean sprouts and mushrooms. Fondue chicken and vegetables to desired doneness. When about one-quarter of chicken remains, add it to fondue pot. Simmer for several minutes, then add noodles of your choice (soaked or precooked). Serve as soup to end the meal.

Make ahead

Prepare broth in advance. At meal time, bring broth to a boil and transfer to fondue pot.

Slice up chicken in advance.

Prepare marinade and marinate chicken for several hours. Keep refrigerated until needed.

Serve with...

Thai peanut sauce, sweet Thai dip, chili garlic sauce.

Dry rub

2 tsp	grated lemon zest	10 mL
2 tsp	lemon pepper	10 mL
1 tsp	garlic powder	5 mL
½ tsp	salt	2 mL
¼ tsp	freshly ground black pepper	1 mL
1 lb	boneless skinless chicken breasts, thinly sliced and cut into 1-inch (2.5 cm) strips	500 g

Broth

5 cups	chicken broth (store-bought or see recipe, page 127)	1.25 L
2	stalks lemon grass, chopped (see tip, page 154)	2
2	green onions, minced	2
1	clove garlic, minced	1
2 tbsp	chopped fresh mint	25 mL
1 tsp	fish sauce	5 mL
½ tsp	granulated sugar	2 mL
¼ tsp	hot pepper flakes	1 mL

1. *Dry rub:* In a small bowl, combine lemon zest, lemon pepper, garlic powder, salt and black pepper; mix well.

2. In a shallow casserole, coat chicken with dry rub, making sure that all pieces are well coated. Cover and refrigerate for at least 1 hour.

3. *Broth:* In a large saucepan, combine chicken broth, lemon grass, green onions, garlic, mint, fish sauce, sugar and hot pepper flakes; mix well. Bring to a boil. Reduce heat and simmer, covered, for 30 minutes. Transfer to fondue pot, setting flame to keep at a simmer.

4. Spear chicken with fondue fork and fondue for 2 to 4 minutes or until cooked through.

Three-Herb Italian Broth Fondue

Marinade

2	cloves garlic, minced	2
1½ tbsp	chopped fresh rosemary	22 mL
1 tbsp	white wine vinegar	15 mL
1 tbsp	water	15 mL
1 tbsp	olive oil	15 mL
	Salt and freshly ground black pepper to taste	
1 lb	boneless skinless chicken breasts, thinly sliced and cut into 1-inch (2.5 cm) strips	500 g

Broth

1 tbsp	olive oil	15 mL
2	shallots, minced	2
2	cloves garlic, minced	2
5 cups	chicken broth (store-bought or see recipe, page 127)	1.25 L
2 tbsp	chopped fresh basil	25 mL
2 tbsp	chopped fresh oregano	25 mL
2 tbsp	chopped fresh parsley	25 mL

1. *Marinade:* In a bowl, whisk together garlic, rosemary, vinegar, water, olive oil, salt and pepper. Mix well.

2. In a shallow casserole, cover chicken strips with marinade, tossing to coat well. Cover and refrigerate for at least 1 hour.

3. *Broth:* In a large saucepan, heat oil over medium heat. Add shallots and garlic; sauté until softened. Add chicken broth, basil, oregano and parsley. Bring to a boil. Reduce heat and simmer, covered, for 15 minutes. Immediately transfer to fondue pot, setting flame to keep at a simmer.

4. Remove chicken strip from marinade, roll and spear with fondue fork. Fondue for 2 to 4 minutes or until cooked through.

Tips

Fresh herbs provide a more intense, more desirable flavor in this fondue.

To turn this fondue into a meal, serve with a vegetable platter consisting of mushrooms, sliced red and green bell peppers, zucchini slices and broccoli florets. Fondue vegetables to desired doneness. When about one-quarter of the chicken remains, add it and any remaining vegetables to fondue pot. Simmer for several minutes, then add cooked vermicelli or orzo. Serve as a soup to end the meal.

Make ahead

Broth can be prepared in advance and then boiled on the stovetop prior to transferring to fondue pot.

Serve with...

Gremolata, roasted red pepper dip, sweet mustard dip.

Cilantro Clam Broth
with Scallops and Shrimp

Tip

As with all broth fondues, the cooking liquid here can also be enjoyed as a soup at the end of the meal. Add any remaining seafood to broth, along with a bunch of cilantro, chopped. (If you wish, spice up the broth with sweet chili sauce.) Add soaked and drained rice stick noodles and cook for 3 to 5 minutes. Enjoy immediately or save for lunch the next day!

Make ahead

Prepare shrimp by peeling and deveining, and cut salmon fillet into pieces. Refrigerate until needed.

Prepare cilantro clam broth up to the end of Step 1. At dinner time, simply carry on with Step 2 and the fondue will be ready in no time at all.

Serve with...

Japanese soy sauce, sweet chili sauce, lemon dill dip, tangy shrimp cocktail sauce.

Broth

1 tbsp	olive oil	15 mL
1	small onion, chopped	1
2	cloves garlic, minced	2
½ cup	dry white wine	125 mL
1	can (5 oz/142 g) baby clams, with broth	1
2 cups	vegetable broth (see recipe, page 130)	500 mL
½ tsp	salt	2 mL
	Freshly ground black pepper to taste	
¾ cup	chopped fresh cilantro	175 mL
1½ tsp	butter	7 mL
½ to 1 tsp	hot pepper sauce	2 to 5 mL
	Chopped fresh parsley for garnish	
8 to 12 oz	shrimp, peeled and deveined	250 to 375 g
8 to 12 oz	scallops or salmon fillet pieces	250 to 375 g

1. *Broth:* In a large saucepan, heat oil over medium heat. Add onion and garlic; sauté for 2 minutes or until softened. Add wine and simmer, uncovered, for 5 minutes or until slightly reduced. Add clams (with broth), vegetable broth, salt and black pepper; simmer, covered, for 10 minutes. Add cilantro, butter and hot pepper sauce; bring to a boil. Reduce heat and simmer for 10 minutes to allow flavors to blend.

2. Transfer broth to fondue pot, setting flame to keep at a simmer. Garnish with parsley.

3. Spear shrimp or scallop (or salmon piece) with fondue fork and fondue for 2 to 4 minutes or until cooked through.

Lemon Honey Dill Scallops Fondue

Marinade

⅓ cup	freshly squeezed lemon juice	75 mL
⅓ cup	liquid honey	75 mL
1 tbsp	olive oil	15 mL
¼ cup	chopped fresh dill	50 mL
	Salt and freshly ground black pepper to taste	
1 lb	scallops	500 g

Broth

5 cups	vegetable broth (store-bought or see recipe, page 130)	1.25 L

1. *Marinade:* In a bowl, whisk together lemon juice, honey, olive oil, dill, salt and pepper.

2. In a shallow casserole, cover scallops with marinade, tossing gently to coat well. Cover and refrigerate for up to 1 hour, turning scallops occasionally.

3. *Broth:* In a large saucepan, bring vegetable broth to a boil. Immediately transfer to fondue pot, setting flame to keep at a simmer.

4. Remove scallop from marinade and spear with fondue fork. Fondue for 1 to 2 minutes or until cooked through.

Serves 4

Tip
To turn this fondue into a meal, serve with a vegetable platter consisting of sliced red and green bell peppers and broccoli florets. Fondue vegetables to desired doneness. When about one-quarter of the scallops remain, add them and any remaining vegetables to fondue pot. Simmer for several minutes, then add soaked and drained rice stick noodles and a dash of hot pepper sauce, if desired. Serve as a soup to end the meal.

Serve with...
Tzatziki, shrimp cocktail sauce, honey mustard.

Scallop Bundles

Marinade

2 tbsp	olive oil	25 mL
2 tbsp	dry white wine	25 mL
2	cloves garlic, minced	2
2 tsp	freshly squeezed lime juice	10 mL
1 tsp	Dijon mustard	5 mL
½ tsp	minced lime zest	2 mL
½ tsp	paprika	2 mL
Pinch	cayenne pepper	Pinch
1 lb	scallops	500 g

Broth

5 cups	vegetable broth (store-bought or see recipe, page 130)	1.25 L
16 to 20	rice wraps (6-inch/15 cm size), soaked and dried (see tip, at left)	16 to 20
	Hoisin sauce	
1	green bell pepper, thinly sliced	1
1	yellow bell pepper, thinly sliced	1
½ cup	shredded daikon radish	125 mL
	Chili garlic sauce (optional)	

1. *Marinade:* In a bowl, combine oil, wine, garlic, lemon juice, Dijon mustard, lime zest, paprika and cayenne; mix well.

2. In a shallow casserole, cover scallops with marinade, tossing gently to coat well. Cover and refrigerate for at least 1 hour.

3. *Broth:* In a large saucepan, bring vegetable broth to a boil. Immediately transfer to fondue pot, setting flame to keep at a simmer.

4. Remove scallops from marinade and spear with fondue fork. Fondue for 2 minutes or until cooked through.

5. *Assembly:* Place rice wrap on plate and spread some hoisin sauce on the upper half. Place 2 scallops on sauce-covered half and top with strips of pepper and a small amount of shredded daikon radish. Season with chili garlic sauce, if desired. Fold up bottom of rice wrap, fold over one side and then the other, leaving the top open. Enjoy!

Make ahead

Prepare marinade in advance and marinate scallops for several hours before the fondue meal.

Serve with...

Hoisin sauce, chili garlic paste, Asian dipping sauce.

Scallops à la Coquilles St. Jacques

Tips

Try a half-and-half combination of scallops and shrimp with this recipe.

If any seafood and white sauce happen to be left over, simply cook the seafood in broth and then add to white sauce. This makes a wonderful filling for crêpes. It's also delicious served on linguine with a sprinkling of freshly grated Parmesan.

Make ahead

Broth can be prepared in advance and then boiled on the stovetop prior to transferring to fondue pot.

Serve with...

Pasta and steamed vegetables.

Broth

5 cups	chicken broth (store-bought or see recipe, page 127)	1.25 L
1/3 cup	dry white wine	75 mL
1 cup	sliced mushrooms	250 mL
1	shallot, minced	1
1/2 tsp	dried thyme	2 mL
1/2 cup	chopped fresh parsley	125 mL

White sauce

1 1/2 cups	half-and-half (10%) cream	375 mL
3 tbsp	butter	45 mL
1/2 tsp	salt	2 mL
3 tbsp	all-purpose flour	45 mL
1 lb	scallops	500 g

1. *Broth:* In a large saucepan, combine chicken broth, wine, mushrooms, shallot and thyme. Bring to a boil. Reduce heat and simmer, covered, for 15 minutes to allow flavors to blend. Transfer to fondue pot, setting flame to keep at a simmer. Garnish broth with parsley.

2. *White sauce:* In a medium saucepan over low heat, combine cream and butter; cook, stirring, until butter is melted and cream is warm. Add salt. Whisk in flour, a little at a time. Continue whisking until smooth. Remove from heat and divide white sauce between 4 individual dipping bowls.

3. Spear a scallop with fondue fork and fondue for 2 minutes or until cooked through. Immediately dip in white sauce.

Lime and Chipotle Shrimp Fondue

Marinade

2	cloves garlic, finely minced	2
1/3 cup	freshly squeezed lime juice	75 mL
1/4 cup	chopped fresh cilantro	50 mL
1 tbsp	finely minced chipotle in adobo sauce (see tips, page 51)	15 mL
	Salt and freshly ground black pepper to taste	
1 lb	shrimp, peeled and deveined	500 g

Broth

5 cups	vegetable broth (store-bought or see recipe, page 130)	1.25 L

1. *Marinade:* In a bowl, whisk together garlic, lime juice, cilantro, chipotle, salt and pepper.

2. In a shallow casserole, cover shrimp with marinade, tossing gently to coat well. Cover and refrigerate for at least 1 hour, turning shrimp occasionally.

3. *Broth:* In a large saucepan, bring vegetable broth to a boil. Immediately transfer to fondue pot, setting flame to keep at a simmer.

4. Remove shrimp from marinade and spear with fondue fork. Fondue for 1 to 2 minutes or until cooked through.

Serves 4

Make ahead
Prepare marinade in advance and marinate shrimp for several hours before the fondue meal.

Serve with...
Tzatziki, shrimp cocktail sauce, cilantro coulis.

Shrimp in Mexican Broth

Tip

To turn this fondue into a meal, serve with a vegetable platter consisting of mushrooms, sliced bell peppers, zucchini slices, broccoli florets and cauliflower florets. Fondue vegetables to desired doneness. When about one-quarter of the shrimp remain, add them and any remaining vegetables to fondue pot. Simmer for several minutes, then add cooked egg noodles and a dash of hot pepper sauce, if desired. Serve as a soup to end the meal.

Make ahead

Peppers can be roasted in advance.

Broth can be prepared in advance and then boiled on the stovetop prior to transferring to fondue pot.

Serve with...

Shrimp cocktail sauce, salsa verde, mango salsa.

Broth

1	jalapeño pepper	1
1	red bell pepper	1
5 cups	chicken or vegetable broth (store-bought or see recipes, page 127 and 130)	1.25 L
2/3 cup	chopped fresh cilantro	150 mL
1/2 cup	chopped onions	125 mL
1/2 cup	Mexican beer (such as Corona)	125 mL
2	cloves garlic, minced	2
4 to 6	drops hot pepper sauce	4 to 6
1 lb	shrimp, peeled and deveined	500 g

1. *Broth:* Preheat broiler. Place jalapeño and red pepper on a broiling pan and broil, turning often, for about 20 minutes or until peppers have blackened all over. Place peppers in a saucepan with a tight-fitting lid for 5 to 10 minutes. Peel and seed both peppers. Cut red pepper in half, mincing half of it and reserving the remainder for another use. Mince jalapeño pepper.

2. In a large saucepan, combine broth, cilantro, onions, beer, garlic, jalapeño, red pepper and hot pepper sauce. Bring to a boil. Reduce heat and simmer, covered, for 15 minutes. Immediately transfer to fondue pot, setting flame to keep at a simmer.

3. Spear shrimp with fondue fork. Fondue for 1 to 2 minutes or until cooked through.

Vietnamese Lemon Grass Shrimp Fondue

Marinade

1 tbsp	vegetable oil	15 mL
1 tbsp	fish sauce	15 mL
3	green onions, minced	3
1	clove garlic, minced	1
3 tbsp	chopped roasted peanuts	45 mL
2	stalks lemon grass, minced (see tip, page 154)	2
1 tsp	granulated sugar	5 mL
½ tsp	hot pepper flakes	2 mL
½ tsp	salt	2 mL
¼ tsp	freshly ground black pepper	1 mL
1 lb	shrimp, peeled and deveined	500 g

Broth

5 cups	chicken broth (store-bought or see recipe, page 127)	1.25 L

Serves 4

Tip
Fish sauce is widely used in Vietnamese and Thai dishes. It has a salty taste and a pungent aroma that may take some getting used to. You can find fish sauce in Asian markets and the Asian food section of larger supermarkets

Make ahead
Prepare marinade in advance and marinate shrimp for several hours before mealtime.

Serve with...
Salsa verde, chili vinegar, Asian dipping sauce, Thai peanut sauce.

1. *Marinade:* In a food processor combine oil, fish sauce, green onions, garlic, peanuts, lemon grass, sugar, hot pepper flakes, salt and black pepper; pulse on and off to form a paste.

2. In a shallow casserole, brush shrimp with marinade, ensuring all are well coated. Cover and refrigerate for at least 1 hour.

3. *Broth:* In a large saucepan, bring chicken broth to a boil. Immediately transfer to fondue pot, setting flame to keep at a simmer.

4. Remove shrimp from marinade and spear with fondue fork. Fondue for 2 minutes or until cooked through.

Lemon Coriander Tuna Fondue

This is a remarkably easy, yet extremely tasty fondue — and low in fat!

Tips
Most fish are not firm enough to survive the fondue pot without falling apart. The exceptions are tuna, halibut and salmon. In this dish, halibut can be used in place of tuna steaks.

Ground coriander gives this dish an unusual, but pleasant flavor. If you are unfamiliar with this spice (or are unable to find it), you can use ground caraway seed instead — although the results will not be as outstanding.

Make ahead
Prepare marinade in advance and marinate tuna steak for several hours.

Serve with...
Wasabi mayonnaise, tartar sauce, shrimp cocktail sauce, honey dill dip.

Marinade

1 tsp	finely grated lemon zest	5 mL
¼ cup	freshly squeezed lemon juice	50 mL
2	cloves garlic, minced	2
2 tbsp	olive oil	25 mL
1 tsp	ground coriander	5 mL
¼ tsp	dried rosemary	1 mL
¼ tsp	dried thyme	1 mL
1 lb	tuna steaks, cut into 1-inch (2.5 cm) cubes	500 mL

Broth

3 cups	fish or vegetable broth (store-bought or see recipes, pages 129 and 130)	750 mL

1. *Marinade:* In a bowl, combine lemon zest, lemon juice, garlic, oil, coriander, rosemary and thyme; mix well.

2. In a shallow casserole, cover tuna pieces with marinade, tossing to coat well. Cover and refrigerate for at least 1 hour.

3. *Broth:* In a large saucepan, bring fish broth to a boil. Immediately transfer to fondue pot, setting flame to keep at a simmer.

4. Remove tuna from marinade and spear with fondue fork. Fondue for 2 to 4 minutes or until cooked through.

Bagna Cauda

6	cloves garlic	6
1	can (1.8 oz/50 g) anchovies, with liquid	1
½ cup	olive oil	125 mL
2 tbsp	butter	25 mL
	Freshly ground black pepper to taste	
	Blanched fennel bulb slices, zucchini slices, broccoli florets or cauliflower florets (see tip, at right)	
	Mushrooms and sliced bell peppers (raw or roasted)	
	Chunks of French bread or focaccia, or pita bread wedges	

1. In a food processor or mini-chopper, mince garlic. Add anchovies, with liquid, and process until finely minced.

2. In a medium saucepan over medium-low heat, bring garlic mixture, olive oil and butter to a simmer, stirring frequently. Sprinkle with pepper. Simmer for 5 minutes to allow flavors to combine. Immediately transfer to fondue pot, setting flame to keep at a simmer.

3. Spear a vegetable or a piece of bread with fondue fork and dip in simmering Bagna Cauda.

Serves 4

This Italian specialty originated in the Piedmont region and is peasant food at its best.

Tip
To blanch vegetables, immerse in a pot of boiling water and cook, uncovered, for about 5 minutes or until tender-crisp. Refresh under cold water to stop cooking. Drain.

Make ahead
Slice vegetables.

Serve with...
Red pepper aïoli, gremolata, salsa verde.

Ginger Tofu in Broth

Serves 4 to 6

This is a great low-fat recipe for vegetarians — and a flavorful surprise for those carnivores who think they don't like tofu.

Tips

If you have leftover tofu cubes, stir-fry them with onions, mushrooms, zucchini and any other vegetables on hand. Serve over basmati rice for a wonderful meal.

Marinades used for raw meat and chicken must be discarded since they contain potentially harmful bacteria. This is not the case for tofu marinades, however, which can be used (as the marinade is in this recipe) for a delicious dipping sauce.

Make ahead

Prepare marinade in advance and marinate tofu earlier in the day. At fondue time, simply bring vegetable broth to a boil, transfer to fondue pot and enjoy.

Serve with...

Marinade and dips such as toasted sesame seeds and sweet-and-sour sauce.

Marinade

¼ cup	soy sauce	50 mL
2 tbsp	minced gingerroot	25 mL
2 tbsp	granulated sugar	25 mL
1 tbsp	sesame oil	15 mL
12 oz	extra-firm tofu, cubed	375 g

Broth

5 cups	vegetable broth (store-bought or see recipe, page 130)	1.25 L

1. *Marinade:* In a bowl, whisk together soy sauce, ginger, sugar and sesame oil.

2. In a shallow casserole, cover tofu with marinade, tossing gently to coat well. Cover and refrigerate for at least 1 hour.

3. *Broth:* In a large saucepan, bring vegetable broth to a boil. Immediately transfer to fondue pot, setting flame to keep at a simmer.

4. With a slotted spoon, transfer tofu to a plate. Pour remaining marinade into small bowls to use as a dipping sauce. Spear tofu with fondue fork and fondue for 3 minutes or until cooked through. Dip in marinade and/or other dipping sauces.

Mongolian Hot Pot (page 160)

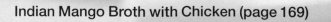
Indian Mango Broth with Chicken (page 169)

Pesto Chicken Fondue (page 173)

Spicy Thai Fondue with Coconut Milk (page 176)

Cilantro Clam Broth with Scallops and Shrimp (page 182)
[salmon variation shown] with Lemon Dill Dip (page 243)

Scallop Bundles (page 184)

Black and White Chocolate Fondue (page 200)

Kids' Favorite Chocolate Fondue (page 214)

Marinated Tofu in Vegetable Broth

Marinade

¼ cup	tamari soy sauce	50 mL
2	green onions, minced	2
1	clove garlic minced	1
1 tbsp	minced gingerroot	15 mL
2 tbsp	dry sherry	25 mL
1 tbsp	rice vinegar	15 mL
1 tbsp	sesame oil	15 mL
Pinch	cayenne pepper	Pinch
12 oz	extra-firm tofu, cubed	375 g

Broth

5 cups	vegetable broth (store-bought or see recipe, page 130)	1.25 L

1. *Marinade:* In a bowl, combine soy sauce, green onions, garlic, ginger, sherry, vinegar, sesame oil and cayenne pepper; mix well

2. In a shallow casserole, cover tofu with marinade, tossing gently to coat well. Cover and refrigerate for at least 1 hour.

3. *Broth:* In a large saucepan, bring vegetable broth to a boil. Immediately transfer to fondue pot, setting flame to keep at a simmer.

4. With a slotted spoon, transfer tofu to a plate. Pour remaining marinade into small bowls to use as a dipping sauce. Spear tofu with fondue fork and fondue for 3 minutes or until cooked through. Dip in marinade and/or other dipping sauces.

Serves 4

Tofu (or bean curd) is a high-protein, low-fat food made from soybeans. It is a good source of calcium, iron, phosphorus, potassium, B vitamins and vitamin E.

Tips

Extra-firm tofu is a must for fonduing. Other types will fall apart in the broth.

Tamari soy sauce, known for its rich color and flavor, is made with soybeans and rice. It contains little or no wheat, making it a good choice for people who do not tolerate gluten in their diet.

To give an extra flavor dimension to the vegetable broth, add 1 tbsp (15 mL) miso paste and ½ tsp (2 mL) sesame oil before bringing it to a boil.

Make ahead

Prepare marinade in advance and marinate tofu cubes until required.

Serve with...

Peanut sauce, marinade, plum sauce.

Dessert fondues

Dessert fondues

Ingredients

DESSERT FONDUES ARE ONE OF the most pleasurable and popular of all fondues. And there's more to this category than the classic chocolate fondue. As you'll discover in this chapter, there are many other sweet treats that will appeal to dessert lovers and serve as a memorable finale to a fabulous fondue meal.

That being said, chocolate is probably the most popular of all fondues. And the most important thing to remember here is to use the best chocolate you can find. Premium brands include Callebaut, Lindt and Valrohna. The same goes for white chocolate (although it isn't really chocolate): use premium brands and you will taste the difference.

Preparing the fondue

CHOCOLATE FONDUES ARE BEST PREPARED right before serving. Most will not take more than 5 to 10 minutes to execute. Some of the desserts in this chapter, such as Butterscotch Fondue (page 224) or Cherries Jubilee Fondue (page 233), can be prepared earlier in the day and then reheated for dessert time.

Melting chocolate is best performed on top of a double boiler over hot (not boiling) water. You can use your microwave on Medium, but you must know your microwave's power and check it every minute or so. When melting chocolate in the microwave, remove it from the microwave before it is completely melted and stir until smooth.

Always melt chocolate with another ingredient, such as cream or butter. If using cream, it should be warmed up before adding the chocolate. It is easier to melt chocolate more evenly when the chocolate is chopped into small pieces rather than large squares.

If chocolate seizes or burns — usually as a result of too high a melting temperature — it becomes grainy. It cannot be salvaged.

If the fondue is too thin, allow it to simmer for a few minutes until it reaches the desired thickness. If it is too thick, stir in liqueur, fruit juice or cream, 1 tbsp (15 mL) at a time, until the consistency is right.

In the fondue pot

ALWAYS USE A FONDUE POT designed specifically for desserts. These ceramic or earthenware pots are smaller than those used for cheese fondues, and they are heated gently by a votive candle, not an alcohol burner. The small candle provides sufficient heat to keep the fondue warm but not so much heat as to cause scorching.

Serving the fondue

FRESH FRUIT IS THE BEST COMPLEMENT to most dessert fondues — especially chocolate. Try the following fruits for success: strawberries, bananas, mango, kiwi, tart apples, pears, seedless grapes, nectarines, honeydew, pineapple, pitted cherries, and cantaloupe.

In addition to fresh fruit, other ideal dippers include ladyfingers, shortbread cookies, sugar cookies, sponge cake, angel food cake, pound cake, banana bread, chocolate cupcakes (for non-chocolate fondues), pretzels, popcorn, nuts, marshmallows and leftover French bread (from the cheese fondue). Maraschino cherries, oranges, dried apricots and dried apples are also delicious when dipped in dessert fondues.

Most of the fruit, cake and other dippers can be cut up and ready to serve in advance of the fondue party. Sprinkle lemon juice on apples and pears to prevent browning. Bananas should be cut up only just before serving.

B-52 Chocolate Fondue

This fondue is perfect company fare. Your guests will love the combination of three liqueurs with dark chocolate.

Make ahead

Chop chocolate.

Cut up fruit and other dippers (except for bananas).

Serve with...

Pineapple chunks, banana slices, mango pieces, melon cubes, dried apricots, strawberries, pretzels, ladyfingers.

⅔ cup + 1 tbsp	whipping (35%) cream	165 mL
12 oz	dark chocolate, chopped	375 g
1 tbsp	Kahlúa	15 mL
1 tbsp	Grand Marnier	15 mL
1 tbsp	Bailey's	15 mL

1. In the top of a double boiler over hot (not boiling) water, heat cream until warm. Add chocolate, stirring constantly until melted and smooth. Remove from heat. Stir in Kahlúa, Grand Marnier and Bailey's. Transfer immediately to dessert fondue pot over candle flame.

2. Spear a piece of fruit or cake with fondue fork and dip in fondue.

Bittersweet Chocolate Fondue

1 cup	whipping (35%) cream	250 mL
8 oz	bittersweet chocolate, chopped	250 g
2 tbsp	Grand Marnier or amaretto or other liqueur	25 mL

1. In the top of a double boiler, over hot (not boiling) water, heat cream until warm. Add chocolate, stirring constantly until melted and smooth. Remove from heat. Stir in liqueur and transfer immediately to dessert fondue pot over candle flame.

2. Spear a piece of fruit or cake with fondue fork and dip in fondue.

Serves 4 to 6

Tip
Always use premium chocolate for fondue — it makes a big difference!

Make ahead
Chop chocolate.

Cut up fruit and other dippers (except for banana). Sprinkle lemon juice on apple wedges.

Serve with...
Whole strawberries, kiwi slices, apple wedges, banana bread chunks.

Black and White Chocolate Fondue

Can't decide? This fondue will suit every chocolate aficionado.

Make ahead

Chop chocolate.

Cut up fruit and other dippers (except for bananas.) Sprinkle lemon juice on apple wedges.

Serve with...

Strawberries, orange slices, banana slices, Granny Smith apple wedges, pretzels, ladyfingers, pound cake cubes.

¾ cup	whipping (35%) cream	375 mL
8 oz	white chocolate, chopped	250 g
1 tsp	vanilla	5 mL
1 tbsp	Kahlúa or other liqueur	25 mL
4 oz	semisweet chocolate chips	125 g

1. In the top of a double boiler over hot (not boiling) water, heat cream until warm. Add white chocolate, stirring constantly until melted and smooth. Remove from heat. Stir in vanilla and Kahlúa. Transfer immediately to dessert fondue pot over candle flame. Stir in chocolate chips with a butter knife to create a swirl effect.

2. Spear a piece of fruit or cake with fondue fork and dip in fondue.

Child-Friendly Orange Chocolate Fondue

½ cup	whipping (35 %) cream	125 mL
8 oz	semisweet chocolate, chopped	250 g
1 tsp	grated orange zest	5 mL
2 tbsp	freshly squeezed orange juice	25 mL

1. In the top of a double boiler over hot (not boiling) water, heat cream until warm. Add chocolate, stirring constantly until melted and smooth. Remove from heat. Stir in orange zest and orange juice. Transfer immediately to dessert fondue pot over candle flame.

2. Spear a piece of fruit or cake with fondue fork and dip in fondue.

Serves 4

The combination of orange and chocolate is wonderful.

Tip
This is intentionally a kid-friendly non-alcoholic fondue, but you may use Grand Marnier or Sabra in place of the fresh orange juice, if desired.

Make ahead
Chop chocolate.

Cut up fruit and other dippers (except for bananas). Sprinkle lemon juice on apple wedges.

Serve with...
Pineapple chunks, banana slices, apple wedges, banana cake cubes, ladyfingers, graham wafers.

Chocolate Butterscotch Fondue

Serves 4 to 6

Tips

If you find the fondue is too thick, stir in additional tablespoon of warmed half-and-half (10%) cream or liqueur.

This fondue is best prepared just before serving.

Make ahead

Chop roasted cashews.

Cut up fruit and other dippers (except for banana).

Serve with...

Pineapple chunks, strawberries, banana, sponge cake cubes, pretzels.

8 oz	chocolate chips	250 g
8 oz	butterscotch chips	250 g
2 tbsp	half-and-half (10%) cream	25 mL
1 tbsp	Kahlúa or other liqueur	15 mL
½ cup	chopped roasted cashews	125 mL

1. In the top of a double boiler over hot (not boiling) water, melt together chocolate chips, butterscotch chips and cream, stirring constantly until smooth. Remove from heat. Stir in Kahlúa and transfer immediately to dessert fondue pot over candle flame. Stir in cashews.

2. Spear a piece of fruit or cake with fondue fork and dip in fondue.

Chocolate Cherry Fondue

½ cup	whipping (35%) cream	125 mL
8 oz	semisweet chocolate, chopped	250 g
1 tbsp	kirsch or other liqueur	15 mL
½ cup	dried sour cherries	125 mL

1. In the top of a double boiler over hot (not boiling) water, heat cream until warm. Add chocolate, stirring constantly until melted and smooth. Remove from heat. Stir in liqueur, then stir in cherries. Transfer immediately to dessert fondue pot over candle flame.

2. Spear a piece of fruit or cake with fondue fork and dip in fondue.

Serves 4

Dried sour cherries are irresistible paired with chocolate. Their tartness takes this fondue up a notch.

Tip
You may use dried cranberries in place of the dried sour cherries.

Make ahead
Chop chocolate.

Cut up fruit and other dippers (except for bananas).

Serve with...
Strawberries, pineapple chunks, banana slices, walnut bread chunks, pound cake cubes, marshmallows, ladyfingers, graham wafers, vanilla wafers.

Chocolate Coconut Fondue

8 oz	semisweet chocolate, chopped	250 g
1/3 cup	evaporated milk	75 mL
2 tbsp	Tia Maria or other liqueur	25 mL
2 tbsp	shredded unsweetened coconut, toasted	25 mL

1. In the top of a double boiler over hot (not boiling) water, melt chocolate with evaporated milk, stirring constantly until smooth. Remove from heat. Stir in liqueur and transfer immediately to dessert fondue pot over candle flame. Stir in coconut; mix well.

2. Spear a piece of fruit or cake with fondue fork and dip in fondue.

Chocolate Fondue
with Pomegranate Seeds

¾ cup	whipping (35%) cream	175 mL
12 oz	milk chocolate, chopped	375 g
1 tbsp	pomegranate juice	15 mL
1 tbsp	grenadine	15 mL
½ cup	pomegranate seeds	125 mL

1. In the top of a double boiler over hot (not boiling) water, heat cream until warm. Add chocolate, stirring constantly until melted and smooth. Remove from heat. Stir in pomegranate juice, grenadine and pomegranate seeds. Transfer immediately to dessert fondue pot over candle flame.

2. Spear a piece of fruit or cake with fondue fork and dip in fondue.

Serves 4

Pomegranate seeds are the latest antioxidant to gain notice. The ruby red, tart seeds of the pomegranate are vitamin-packed nutritional powerhouses.

Tip
If desired, use 2 tbsp (25 mL) of pomegranate juice or grenadine instead of 1 tbsp (15 mL) of each.

Make ahead
Chop chocolate.

Seed pomegranate. For best results, slice in half and immerse cut half in water, removing seeds by hand.

Cut up fruit and other dippers (except for bananas).

Serve with...
Blackberries, strawberries, banana slices, dried apricots, dates, shortbread cookies, ladyfingers.

Chocolate Marshmallow Fondue

Tips

Be sure to use unsweetened baking chocolate for this fondue. With the added marshmallows, any other type of chocolate will make the fondue too sweet.

If you use unsweetened chocolate and still find the fondue too sweet, stir in 1 to 2 tsp (5 to 10 mL) freshly squeezed lemon juice before transferring to fondue pot.

Make ahead

Cut up fruit and other dippers.

Serve with...

Nectarine wedges, cantaloupe cubes, seedless grapes, pound cake cubes, shortbread cookies.

2 oz	unsweetened chocolate	60 g
20	marshmallows, quartered	20
6 tbsp	corn syrup	90 mL
2 tbsp	half-and-half (10%) cream	25 mL
1 tbsp	butter, melted	15 mL
1 tsp	vanilla	5 mL

1. In the top of a double boiler over hot (not boiling) water, melt together chocolate, marshmallows, corn syrup and cream, stirring constantly until smooth. Remove from heat. Stir in butter and vanilla. Transfer immediately to dessert fondue pot over candle flame.

2. Spear a piece of fruit or cake with fondue fork and dip in fondue.

Chocolate Mint Fondue

½ cup	whipping (35%) cream	125 mL
8 oz	semisweet chocolate, chopped	250 g
1 tbsp	crème de menthe	15 mL
1 tbsp	finely chopped peppermints	15 mL

1. In the top of a double boiler over hot (not boiling) water, heat cream until warm. Add chocolate, stirring constantly until melted and smooth. Remove from heat. Stir in crème de menthe and transfer immediately to dessert fondue pot over candle flame. Stir in chopped peppermints.

2. Spear a piece of fruit or cake with fondue fork and dip in fondue.

Serves 4

Tip
Decorate fruit and cake platter with mint leaves. Chop up mint leaves for garnish on fondued cake and fruit pieces.

Make ahead
Cut up fruit and other dippers.

Serve with...
Angel food cake cubes, ladyfingers, pineapple chunks, cherries, marshmallows.

Chocolate Peanut Butter Fondue

Peanut butter cups, anyone? Who can resist chocolate and peanut butter?

Make ahead

Chop chocolate.

Cut up fruit and other dippers (except for bananas). Sprinkle lemon juice on apple wedges.

Serve with...
Banana slices, apple wedges, cherries, shortbread cookies, vanilla wafers, marshmallows, pound cake cubes.

¾ cup	whipping (35%) cream	175 mL
⅓ cup	natural crunchy peanut butter	75 mL
8 oz	milk chocolate, chopped	250 g
1 tsp	vanilla	5 mL

1. In the top of a double boiler over hot (not boiling) water, heat cream and peanut butter until cream is warm and peanut butter is softened. Add chocolate, stirring constantly until melted and smooth. Remove from heat. Stir in vanilla and transfer immediately to dessert fondue pot over candle flame.

2. Spear a piece of fruit or cake with fondue fork and dip in fondue

Chocolate Sour Cream Fondue

½ cup	whipping (35%) cream	125 mL
⅓ cup	sour cream	75 mL
12 oz	milk chocolate, chopped	375 g
1 tbsp	crème de cacao or other liqueur	25 mL

1. In a bowl, combine whipping cream and sour cream, stirring until blended. In the top of a double boiler over hot (not boiling) water, heat cream and sour cream until warm. Add chocolate, stirring constantly until melted and smooth. Remove from heat. Stir in liqueur and transfer immediately to dessert fondue pot over candle flame.

2. Spear a piece of fruit or cake with fondue fork and dip in fondue.

Serves 4

This unique fondue is exceptional. The sour cream balances the sweetness of the chocolate for a distinctive, and delectable, taste.

Tip
You may use the liqueur of your choice, but I recommend crème de cacao to add to the rich chocolate flavor.

Make ahead
Chop chocolate.

Cut up fruit and other dippers. Sprinkle lemon juice on pear wedges.

Serve with...
Raspberries, cantaloupe cubes, pineapple chunks, kiwi slices, pear wedges, angel food cake cubes, shortbread cookies, melba toast rounds.

Dark Chocolate Fondue

¾ cup	whipping (35%) cream	175 mL
12 oz	premium dark chocolate, chopped	375 g
2 tbsp	kirsch or Kahlúa or other liqueur	25 mL

Serves 4

Tip

To microwave, heat cream on Medium in microwave-safe bowl until warmed (not boiling). Remove from microwave and stir in chocolate. Stir until melted and smooth. Stir in liqueur and transfer to fondue pot.

Make ahead

Chop chocolate.

Cut up fruit and other dippers (except for banana). Sprinkle lemon juice on apple wedges.

Serve with...

Melon cubes, apple wedges, pineapple chunks, cherries, strawberries, banana slices, orange slices, pound cake cubes, ladyfingers, banana bread chunks, marshmallows.

1. In the top of a double boiler over hot (not boiling) water, heat cream until warm. Add chocolate, stirring constantly until melted and smooth. Remove from heat. Stir in kirsch and transfer immediately to dessert fondue pot over candle flame.

2. Spear a piece of fruit or cake with fondue fork and dip in fondue.

Variations

For different flavors, try the following combinations of liqueur added to the chocolate mixture.

Mocha: *Add 1 tbsp (15 mL) Kahlúa and 1 tsp (5 mL) instant coffee dissolved in another 1 tbsp (15 mL) Kahlúa.*

Orange: *Add 2 tbsp (25 mL) Grand Marnier and 1 tsp (5 mL) minced orange zest.*

Almond: *Add 2 tbsp (25 mL) amaretto, ½ tsp (2 mL) almond extract and 2 tbsp (25 mL) chopped toasted slivered almonds.*

Diabetic Chocolate Fondue

⅔ cup	unsweetened cocoa powder, sifted	150 mL
1 cup	2% evaporated milk	250 mL
2 tbsp	margarine	25 mL
⅔ cup	Splenda	150 mL
1 tbsp	cornstarch	15 mL
1 tsp	vanilla	5 mL
½ cup	chopped walnuts, toasted (optional)	125 mL

1. Stir cocoa powder into evaporated milk. In a medium saucepan, over low heat, melt margarine. Whisk in cocoa powder mixture and Splenda until smooth. Increase heat to medium and whisk in cornstarch until thickened, about 2 minutes (do not boil). Stir in vanilla. Remove from heat and transfer immediately to dessert fondue pot over candle flame. Sprinkle with toasted walnuts, if using.

2. Spear a piece of fruit or angel food cake onto fondue fork and dip in fondue.

This fondue will be appreciated by the increasing number of people living with diabetes, as well as anyone watching their sugar and fat intake. Children, especially, will love it.

Tip
Use high-quality cocoa powder for best results.

Make ahead
Cut up fruit and other dippers (except for bananas). Sprinkle lemon juice on apple and pear wedges.

Serve with...
Banana slices, strawberries, apple wedges, pear wedges, orange sections, sugar-free biscuits, sugar-free angel food cake cubes.

Heavenly Chocolate Fondue

Tip

To chop chocolate, place on a clean cutting board and, with a large chef's knife pointed toward the board, go up and down slowly. Alternatively, grate with coarse grater.

Make ahead

Cut up fruit and other dippers (except for bananas).

Serve with...

Banana slices, strawberries, kiwi slices, honeydew melon cubes, pear wedges, orange sections, graham wafers, pretzels.

¾ cup	whipping (35%) cream	175 mL
12 oz	semisweet chocolate, chopped	375 g
2 tbsp	Kahlúa or amaretto or other liqueur	25 mL

1. In the top of a double boiler over hot (not boiling) water, heat cream until warm. Add chocolate, stirring constantly until melted and smooth. Remove from heat. Stir in Kahlúa and transfer immediately to dessert fondue pot over candle flame.

2. Spear a piece of fruit or cake with fondue fork and dip in fondue.

Honey-Nougat Chocolate Fondue

½ cup	half-and-half (10%) cream	125 mL
1	bar (13 oz/400 g) Swiss honey-nougat chocolate bar, chopped	1
1 tbsp	Kahlúa, cognac or other liqueur	15 mL

1. In a saucepan, heat cream over low heat until warm. Add chocolate bar, stirring constantly until nearly melted. Remove from heat. Continue stirring until melted. Slowly stir in Kahlúa; mix well. Transfer immediately to dessert fondue pot over candle flame.

2. Spear a piece of fruit or cake with fondue fork and dip in fondue.

Serves 4 to 6

This is the perfect cottage fondue. It's easy to make, the ingredients are simple and the results are spectacular.

Make ahead

Cut up fruit and other dippers (except for bananas.) Sprinkle lemon juice on apple and pear wedges.

Serve with...

Strawberries, banana slices, pineapple chunks, cantaloupe cubes, apple wedges, pear wedges, kiwi slices.

Kids' Favorite Chocolate Fondue

Tip
When chocolate is chopped, it melts more evenly.

Make ahead
Chop chocolate.

Cut up fruit and other dippers (except for bananas). Sprinkle lemon juice on apple and pear wedges.

Serve with...
Strawberries, banana slices, orange sections, pear wedges, apple wedges, vanilla wafers, sponge cake cubes, marshmallows, maraschino cherries.

½ cup	whipping (35%) cream	125 mL
8 oz	semisweet chocolate, chopped	250 g
1 tbsp	candy sprinkles	15 mL

1. In the top of a double boiler over hot (not boiling) water, heat cream until warm. Add chocolate, stirring constantly until melted and smooth. Remove from heat and transfer immediately to dessert fondue pot over candle flame. Add sprinkles just before serving.

2. Spear a piece of fruit or cake with fondue fork and dip in fondue.

Mexican Chocolate Fondue

½ cup	whipping (35%) cream	125 mL
8 oz	Mexican or dark chocolate, chopped	250 g
1	cinnamon stick (1 inch/2.5 cm)	1
1 tsp	ground cinnamon	5 mL
¼ tsp	cayenne pepper	1 mL
1 tbsp	tequila or other liqueur (optional)	15 mL

1. In the top of a double boiler over hot (not boiling) water, heat cream until warm. Add chocolate, stirring constantly until melted and smooth. Remove from heat. Stir in cinnamon stick, ground cinnamon, cayenne and tequila (if using). Transfer immediately to dessert fondue pot over candle flame.

2. Spear a piece of fruit or cake with fondue fork and dip in fondue.

Cinnamon gives this fondue an amazing aroma.

Tip
Try to find authentic Mexican chocolate, if possible; if you can't, use a high-quality dark chocolate.

Make ahead
Chop chocolate.

Cut up fruit and other dippers (except for bananas). Sprinkle lemon juice on pear wedges.

Serve with...
Pineapple chunks, banana slices, mango slices, orange sections, pear wedges, whole almonds, coconut chunks, ladyfingers, angel food cake cubes.

Mocha Fudge Fondue

Tips

If fondue is too thick, add more warmed coffee 1 tbsp (15 mL) at a time.

In place of double-strength coffee, use brewed espresso for an intense coffee flavor.

Make ahead

Cut up fruit and other dippers (except for bananas).

Serve with...

Whole strawberries, seedless grapes, peach wedges, banana cake cubes, pound cake cubes.

2 cups	confectioner's (icing) sugar	500 mL
½ cup	whipping (35%) cream	125 mL
¼ cup	double-strength coffee	50 mL
4 oz	semisweet chocolate, chopped	125 g
2 oz	unsweetened chocolate	60 g
1 tbsp	Kahlúa	15 mL
1 tsp	vanilla	5 mL

1. In the top of a double boiler over hot (not boiling) water, combine sugar, cream, coffee, semisweet chocolate and unsweetened chocolate, stirring constantly until melted and smooth. Remove from heat. Stir in Kahlúa and vanilla. Transfer immediately to dessert fondue pot over candle flame.

2. Spear a piece of fruit or cake with fondue fork and dip in fondue.

Nutty Chocolate Fondue

½ cup	half-and-half (10%) cream	125 mL
1 cup	semisweet chocolate chips	250 mL
1 cup	peanut butter chips	250 mL
1 cup	hazelnut chocolate spread	250 mL
2 tbsp	chopped roasted peanuts	25 mL

1. In the top of a double boiler over hot (not boiling) water, heat cream until warm. Add chocolate chips, stirring constantly until melted and smooth. Stir in peanut butter chips and hazelnut chocolate spread until melted and smooth. (If too thick, stir in cream 1 tbsp (15 mL) at a time until desired consistency is reached.) Remove from heat and transfer immediately to dessert fondue pot over candle flame. Stir in chopped peanuts.

2. Spear a piece of fruit or cake with fondue fork and dip in fondue.

Peanut Butter Cherries in Chocolate Fondue

The combination of chocolate, peanut butter and cherries is amazing.

Tip
You can serve this the usual fondue way or do it ahead of time for a special occasion. This recipe is always a hit at showers when the cherries are dipped in chocolate and allowed to cool and harden.

Make ahead

Prepare to end of Step 2. Refrigerate until needed.

Chop chocolate.

Serve with...
Pineapple chunks, strawberries, blackberries, banana slices, kiwi slices, vanilla wafers.

Cherries

½ cup	confectioner's (icing) sugar	125 mL
½ cup	natural crunchy peanut butter	125 mL
¼ cup	graham wafer crumbs	50 mL
1½ tbsp	butter, softened	22 mL
Pinch	salt	Pinch
30	maraschino cherries with stems, drained and patted dry	30

Chocolate fondue

½ cup	whipping (35 %) cream	125 mL
8 oz	dark or milk chocolate, chopped	250 g

1. *Cherries:* In a small bowl, beat together confectioner's sugar, peanut butter, graham wafer crumbs, butter and salt until smooth. Form mixture into a ball. Wrap in plastic wrap and refrigerate for 1 hour.

2. Remove half of the peanut butter mixture and return the other half to the fridge until needed. Roll a cherry-sized amount of peanut butter mixture into a small ball and make an indent in the centre. Place a cherry in the middle of the peanut butter mixture, patting the mixture around the cherry until it is covered. Place on baking sheet lined with parchment paper. Repeat until all cherries are coated, then place baking sheet in the refrigerator.

3. *Chocolate fondue:* In the top of a double boiler over hot (not boiling) water, heat cream until warm. Add chocolate, stirring constantly until melted and smooth. Remove from heat and transfer immediately to dessert fondue pot over candle flame.

4. Hold a cherry by its stem and dip in chocolate fondue. Enjoy right away or let chocolate harden slightly. (You may also spear a piece of fruit or cake with fondue fork and dip in fondue.)

Rocky Road Fondue

8 oz	semisweet chocolate, chopped	250 g
1½ cups	white mini marshmallows	375 mL
¾ cup	half-and-half (10%) cream	175 mL
1 tsp	vanilla	5 mL
1 to 2 tbsp	graham wafer crumbs	15 to 25 mL

1. In the top of a double boiler over simmering (not boiling) water, combine chocolate, marshmallows and cream. Heat, stirring constantly, until chocolate and marshmallows are melted, about 8 minutes. Remove from heat. Stir in vanilla and transfer immediately to dessert fondue pot over candle flame. Sprinkle with graham wafer crumbs.

2. Spear a piece of fruit or cake with fondue fork and dip in fondue.

Serves 4

Tip
You may substitute premium milk chocolate chunks (not chocolate chips) for the semisweet chocolate.

Make ahead
Chop chocolate.

Cut up fruit and other dippers. Sprinkle lemon juice on apple wedges.

Serve with...
Apple wedges, orange sections, pineapple chunks, cantaloupe cubes, ladyfingers, pretzels.

Turtle Fondue

Serves 4

Re-create a favorite chocolate confectionery in your fondue pot.

Make ahead

Chop chocolate.

Unwrap and quarter caramels.

Cut up fruit and other dippers (except for bananas). Sprinkle lemon juice on apple wedges.

Serve with...

Granny Smith apple wedges, strawberries, banana slices, angel food cake cubes, ladyfingers, pretzels, graham wafers.

½ cup	whipping (35%) cream	125 mL
8 oz	semisweet chocolate, chopped	250 g
20	caramels, unwrapped and quartered, divided	20
¼ cup	chopped pecans	50 mL

1. In the top of a double boiler over hot (not boiling) water, heat cream until warm. Add chocolate, stirring constantly. When chocolate is about half melted, gradually start stirring in caramel pieces, a few at a time, reserving about one-quarter of the caramels for later. Continue stirring until chocolate is melted and caramels are softened and swirled throughout the chocolate. Remove from heat and transfer immediately to dessert fondue pot over candle flame. Sprinkle with pecans.

2. Spear a piece of fruit or cake with fondue fork and dip in fondue. Occasionally, as you are dipping, add the remaining caramels to the fondue.

White Chocolate and Macadamia Nut Fondue

½ cup	whipping (35%) cream	125 mL
8 oz	white chocolate, chopped	250 g
1 tbsp	amaretto or other liqueur	15 mL
¼ cup	coarsely chopped macadamia nuts	50 mL

1. In the top of a double boiler over hot (not boiling) water, heat cream until warm. Add white chocolate, stirring constantly until melted and smooth. Remove from heat. Stir in amaretto and transfer immediately to dessert fondue pot over candle flame. Sprinkle with macadamia nuts.

2. Spear a piece of fruit or cake with fondue fork and dip in fondue.

Serves 4

Macadamia nuts and white chocolate are a magical pairing.

Make ahead

Chop chocolate.

Cut up fruit and other dippers. Sprinkle lemon juice on pear wedges.

Serve with...

Pineapple chunks, kiwi slices, mango slices, orange sections, pear wedges, cherries, dried apricots, angel food cake cubes.

White Chocolate and Toffee Fondue

My 11-year-old son, Jesse, thinks this is the best fondue ever — and it's easy enough that he can prepare it himself.

Tip

For a thicker fondue, omit the cream. Just melt the chocolate and stir in the toffee bits. Be sure to stir frequently while fonduing.

Make ahead

Cut up fruit and other dippers (except for bananas).

Serve with...

Banana slices, pineapple chunks, strawberries, mango cubes, kiwi slices, dried cranberries, orange sections, apple wedges, plum wedges, melba toast rounds, pretzels, ladyfingers.

⅓ cup	whipping (35%) cream	75 mL
12 oz	premium white chocolate, chopped	375 g
½ cup	toffee bits	125 mL

1. In the top of a double boiler over hot (not boiling) water, heat cream until warm. Add white chocolate, stirring constantly until melted and smooth. Remove from heat. Stir in toffee bits and transfer immediately to dessert fondue pot over candle flame.

2. Spear a piece of fruit or cake with fondue fork and dip in fondue.

White Chocolate Fondue

½ cup	whipping (35%) cream	125 mL
12 oz	premium white chocolate, chopped	375 g
1½ tsp	coconut rum	7 mL

Serves 4 to 6

1. In the top of a double boiler over hot (not boiling) water, heat cream until warm. Add white chocolate, stirring constantly until melted and smooth. Remove from heat. Stir in coconut rum and transfer immediately to dessert fondue pot over candle flame.

2. Spear a piece of fruit or cake with fondue fork and dip in fondue.

This recipe was given to me by Dustin Hoekstra, co-owner with Leah Sellers of Winnipeg's only fondue restaurant, The Melting Pot. His parents, Cathie and Fokke Hoekstra, originally operated the restaurant under the name The Fork and Cork.

Tip
If you wish, warm cream before adding chocolate.

Make ahead
Chop chocolate.

Cut up fruit and other dippers (except for bananas). Sprinkle lemon juice on pear wedges.

Serve with...
Pineapple chunks, banana slices, dried apricots, pretzels, shortbread cookies, peach wedges, pear wedges, melba toast rounds.

Butterscotch Fondue

Tip

If you wish, replace half-and-half with whipping (35%) cream. Don't try substituting a lighter cream, however; it will make the fondue too thin. Dessert fondues are rarely low in fat!

Make ahead

Prepare fondue to the end of Step 1. Cool, then refrigerate. Reheat in microwave on Low until heated (about 1 to 2 minutes) or over low heat in saucepan on stove. Stir and transfer to fondue pot.

Cut up fruit and other dippers (except for banana) Sprinkle lemon juice on pear wedges.

Serve with...

Pear wedges, banana chunks, pineapple chunks, dried apricots, sponge cake cubes, vanilla wafers.

1½ cups	packed brown sugar	375 mL
½ cup	butter	125 mL
½ cup	half-and-half (10%) cream	125 mL

1. In a saucepan over low heat, combine brown sugar, butter and cream; cook, stirring, for 5 minutes or until sugar dissolves. Increase heat to medium and bring to a boil, stirring occasionally. Boil without stirring for about 7 minutes or until thickened, watching carefully that it does not become too thick.

2. Transfer mixture to dessert fondue pot over candle flame.

3. Spear a piece of fruit or cake with fondue fork and dip in fondue.

Caramel Fondue

1 cup	granulated sugar	250 mL
1 tbsp	cornstarch	15 mL
1 tbsp	rum	15 mL
1 cup	milk, warmed	250 mL
2	egg yolks, beaten	2
¼ cup	boiling water	50 mL
½ tsp	vanilla	2 mL

1. In a large heavy-bottomed skillet over medium heat, melt sugar for 5 to 10 minutes, stirring occasionally at first, then constantly, until sugar is completely liquefied and browned.

2. Meanwhile, in a small bowl, whisk together cornstarch and rum.

3. In the top of a double boiler over hot (not boiling) water, combine milk, egg yolks and cornstarch mixture. Cook, stirring constantly, for 3 to 5 minutes or until smooth.

4. When sugar has caramelized, remove skillet from heat. Carefully stir in boiling water. (Mixture will bubble and spatter.) Immediately pour caramel into warm milk mixture in top of double boiler. Caramel will solidify again, but keep stirring over low heat for about 20 minutes until melted.

5. Remove double boiler from heat; stir in vanilla. Transfer immediately to dessert fondue pot over candle flame.

6. Spear a piece of fruit or cake with fondue fork and dip in fondue.

Serves 4 to 6

Tip
Use a skillet instead of a saucepan to melt the sugar; its cooking surface is larger.

Make ahead
Prepare to end of end of Step 3. Cool, then refrigerate. Reheat in microwave on Low until heated (about 1 to 2 minutes) or over low heat in saucepan on stove. Stir, add vanilla and transfer to fondue pot.

Cut up fruit and other dippers. Sprinkle lemon juice on apple wedges.

Serve with...
Ladyfingers, chocolate cupcake pieces, apple wedges, nectarine wedges, marshmallows.

Quick Caramel Fondue

14 oz	vanilla caramels	425 g
½ cup	light (5%) cream	125 mL
2 tbsp	rum	25 mL

Tips

The caramel may seem a little thin, but it quickly thickens as it cools. Dip pieces of fruit in fondue and hold in the air for a few seconds. The caramel will adhere to the fruit.

If you have leftover caramel fondue, spear a whole apple with fondue fork and dip in sauce. Set on a baking sheet lined with waxed paper to cool in refrigerator.

Make ahead

Prepare to end of Step 1. Cool, then refrigerate. Reheat in microwave on Low until heated (about 1 to 2 minutes) or over low heat in saucepan on stove. Stir and transfer to fondue pot.

Cut up fruit and other dippers (except for bananas.) Sprinkle lemon juice on apple and pear wedges.

Serve with...

Granny Smith apple wedges, pear wedges, banana chunks, pineapple chunks, vanilla wafers, ladyfingers.

1. In the top of a double boiler over hot (not boiling) water, melt together caramels and cream, stirring constantly until smooth. Remove from heat. Stir in rum.

2. Transfer immediately to dessert fondue pot over candle flame.

3. Spear a piece of fruit or cake with fondue fork and dip in fondue.

Maple Fondue

1²∕₃ cups	whipping cream, divided	400 mL
½ cup	pure maple syrup	125 mL
1½ tbsp	cornstarch	22 mL
1 tbsp	butter	15 mL

1. In a medium saucepan, heat 1½ cups (375 mL) of the whipping cream and the maple syrup over low heat for about 12 minutes or until hot and starting to thicken. Whisk together cornstarch and the remaining cream. Increase heat to medium and whisk in cornstarch mixture; cook, whisking constantly, for 1 to 2 minutes or until thickened (do not boil). Whisk in butter until melted.

2. Remove from heat and transfer immediately to dessert fondue pot over candle flame.

3. Spear a piece of fruit or cake with fondue fork and dip in fondue.

Serves 4 to 6

Tip
You must use real maple syrup for this recipe to shine.

Make ahead
Complete to the end of Step 1. Let cool, then refrigerate. Reheat in microwave on Low (1 to 2 minutes) or over low heat in a saucepan on the stovetop. Stir and transfer to fondue pot.

Cut up fruit and other dippers (except for bananas.)

Serve with...
Pineapple chunks, banana slices, mango slices, walnuts, ladyfingers, pound cake cubes.

Maple Walnut Fondue

Serves 4 to 6

If you're like my husband, Ari, who loves maple walnut anything, then this is the fondue for you.

Tip

Walnuts go rancid quickly, so make sure the ones you buy are fresh. You can keep them fresh in refrigerator for up to 6 months or in the freezer for up to 1 year.

Make ahead

Prepare to end of Step 2. Cool, then refrigerate. Reheat in microwave on Low until heated (about 1 to 2 minutes) or over low heat in saucepan on stove. Stir and transfer to fondue pot.

Cut up fruit and other dippers (except for bananas). Sprinkle lemon juice on apple wedges.

Serve with...

Pineapple chunks, banana slices, ladyfingers, mango slices, apple wedges.

²⁄₃ cup	2% evaporated milk	150 mL
½ cup	pure maple syrup	125 mL
6 tbsp	corn syrup	90 mL
1 tbsp	cornstarch	15 mL
2 tbsp	butter	25 mL
½ tsp	vanilla	2 mL
½ cup	chopped walnuts, toasted	125 mL

1. In a saucepan over low heat, combine evaporated milk, maple syrup and corn syrup. Increase heat to medium. Whisk in cornstarch and cook, whisking constantly, for 5 minutes or until thickened. (Do not allow to boil.)

2. Add butter and vanilla; stir until melted and smooth. Transfer immediately to dessert fondue pot over candle flame. Stir in walnuts.

3. Spear a piece of fruit or cake with fondue fork and dip in fondue.

Peanut Butter Fondue

¼ cup	packed brown sugar	50 mL
¼ cup	corn syrup	50 mL
¼ cup	water	50 mL
2 tbsp	butter	25 mL
4	marshmallows	4
⅔ cup	smooth peanut butter	150 mL
½ cup	2% evaporated milk	125 mL
1 tsp	vanilla	5 mL

1. In a saucepan over low heat, combine brown sugar, corn syrup, water and butter; cook, stirring, for 5 minutes or until sugar is dissolved. Add marshmallows, peanut butter and evaporated milk; continue to stir until melted and smooth. Remove from heat and stir in vanilla. Transfer immediately to dessert fondue pot over candle flame. Stir occasionally to prevent excess thickening.

2. Spear a piece of fruit or cake with fondue fork and dip in fondue.

Serves 4 to 6

This is a great fondue for kids (as long as no one has peanut allergies) and will be enjoyed by adults as well.

Tips
Use smooth peanut butter for a creamy consistency.

Once transferred to fondue pot, be sure to stir occasionally to prevent fondue from becoming too thick.

Make ahead
Cut up fruit and other dippers (except for bananas). Sprinkle lemon juice on apple wedges.

Serve with...
Banana slices, apple wedges, pound cake cubes, chocolate biscuit fingers, pretzels, melba toast rounds, strawberries.

Rum and Butter Fondue

This is a delicious fondue that is just as good reheated the next day and served over ice cream.

Tip

If you don't like your desserts too sweet, omit the raisins.

Make ahead

Prepare to end of Step 1. Cool, then refrigerate. Reheat in microwave on Low until heated (about 1 to 2 minutes) or over low heat in saucepan on stove. Stir and transfer to fondue pot.

Cut up fruit and other dippers (except for bananas).

Serve with...

Mango pieces, peach wedges, pineapple chunks, banana slices, dried apricots, ladyfingers, marshmallows, shortbread cookies.

½ cup	packed brown sugar	125 mL
½ cup	corn syrup	125 mL
1 cup	half-and-half (10%) cream, warmed	250 mL
2 tbsp	cornstarch	25 mL
¼ cup	butter, melted	50 mL
2 tbsp	rum	25 mL
¼ cup	raisins (optional)	50 mL

1. In a saucepan over low heat, combine brown sugar and corn syrup; cook, stirring, for 5 minutes or until sugar is dissolved. In a bowl, whisk together cream and cornstarch; whisk into sugar mixture a little at a time. Cook, stirring constantly, until fondue comes to a boil.

2. Remove from heat. Add butter and rum, whisking until smooth. Transfer immediately to dessert fondue pot over candle flame. Stir in raisins if desired.

3. Spear a piece of fruit or cake with fondue fork and dip in fondue.

Vanilla Fondue

¾ cup	granulated sugar	175 mL
4 tsp	cornstarch	20 mL
Pinch	salt	Pinch
1¼ cups	boiling water	300 mL
3 tbsp	unsalted butter, melted	45 mL
1½ tsp	vanilla	7 mL

1. In a saucepan over medium heat, combine sugar, cornstarch and salt. Slowly pour in boiling water, stirring constantly, until mixture comes to a boil. Reduce heat to low and simmer for 5 minutes or until thickened.

2. Remove from heat and stir in melted butter and vanilla. Transfer immediately to dessert fondue pot over candle flame.

3. Spear a piece of fruit or cake with fondue fork and dip in fondue.

Tips
This recipe is easily doubled for a larger group.

If you can find it, use "white" vanilla. This type (which is actually clear) will not darken the color of the fondue.

Make ahead
Prepare to end of Step 1. Cool, then refrigerate. Reheat in microwave on low until heated (about 1 to 2 minutes) or over low heat in saucepan on stove. Stir and transfer to fondue pot.

Cut up fruit and other dippers.

Serve with...
Chocolate cupcake cubes, chocolate finger biscuits, raspberry scone cubes, chocolate pound cake cubes, peach wedges, nectarine wedges, orange sections.

Cheesecake Fondue

Quick, easy and delicious — what more do you want from a dessert fondue?

Make ahead

Cut up fruit and other dippers.

Serve with...

Maraschino cherries, strawberries, kiwi slices, mango pieces, graham wafers, chocolate wafers, chocolate cupcake cubes.

1	package (8 oz/250 g) cream cheese, softened	1
1	jar (6.5 oz/198 g) marshmallow cream	1
2 tbsp	milk	25 mL
1 tsp	freshly squeezed lemon juice	5 mL

1. In saucepan over medium-low heat, combine cream cheese and marshmallow cream; cook, whisking constantly, until cream cheese and marshmallow cream are melted. (Watch carefully to avoid scorching.) Slowly add milk, 1 tbsp (15 mL) at a time, stirring well to combine. Stir in lemon juice; mix well. Remove from heat and transfer immediately to dessert fondue pot over candle flame.

2. Spear a piece of fruit or cake with fondue fork and dip in fondue.

Cherries Jubilee Fondue

2 tbsp	cornstarch	25 mL
2 tbsp	water	25 mL
1	can (14 oz/398 mL) sour cherries, pitted and halved, syrup drained and reserved	1
¼ cup	granulated sugar	50 mL
2 tbsp	kirsch	25 mL
4 tsp	freshly squeezed lemon juice	20 mL

1. In a small bowl, whisk together cornstarch and water.

2. In a saucepan over medium heat, warm reserved cherry syrup. Whisk in dissolved cornstarch and sugar; reduce heat to low and cook, stirring, for 5 minutes or until thickened. Stir in halved cherries; simmer, uncovered, for 20 minutes. Add kirsch and lemon juice; stir well.

3. Transfer immediately to dessert fondue pot over candle flame.

4. Spear a piece of fruit or cake with fondue fork and dip in fondue.

Serves 4 to 6

Tips
If the sauce is too thick, add additional kirsch. If the sauce is too sweet, add extra lemon juice 1 tsp (5 mL) at a time.

For a smoother consistency, purée half of the cherries in food processor and add together with remaining cherries.

Make ahead
Prepare to end of Step 2. Cool, then refrigerate. Reheat in microwave on low until heated (about 1 to 2 minutes) or over low heat in saucepan on stove. Stir in kirsch and transfer to fondue pot.

Cut up fruit and other dippers.

Serve with...
Cubed angel food cake, ladyfingers, strawberries, marshmallows, or over ice cream.

Pineapple Fondue

Serves 4 to 6

Tips
For a more intense cinnamon flavor, increase the amount of the spice to 1/2 tsp (2 mL).

Try using another fruit-flavored liqueur instead of the Grand Marnier.

Make ahead
Prepare to end of Step 1. Cool, then refrigerate. Reheat in microwave on low until heated (about 1 to 2 minutes) or over low heat in saucepan on stove. Stir and transfer to fondue pot.

Cut up fruit and other dippers (except for bananas.)

Serve with...
Angel food cake cubes, banana bread cubes, ladyfingers, banana slices, kiwi slices, dried apricots.

1 cup	pineapple juice	250 mL
3/4 cup	crushed pineapple, drained, 1/4 cup (50 mL) syrup reserved	175 mL
1/4 cup	granulated sugar	50 mL
2 tbsp	cornstarch	25 mL
1 tbsp	freshly squeezed lemon juice	15 mL
1/4 tsp	ground cinnamon	1 mL
4 tsp	Grand Marnier	20 mL

1. In the top of a double boiler over boiling water, combine pineapple juice, reserved pineapple syrup, sugar and cornstarch; cook, stirring constantly, for 3 to 5 minutes or until thickened.

2. Remove from heat. Stir in lemon juice, cinnamon and crushed pineapple. Stir in Grand Marnier. Transfer immediately to dessert fondue pot over candle flame.

3. Spear a piece of fruit or cake with fondue fork and dip in fondue.

Hawaiian Fondue

½ cup	butter	125 mL
1 cup	packed brown sugar	250 mL
⅔ cup	pineapple juice	150 mL
2 tbsp	rum	25 mL
¼ tsp	ground nutmeg	1 mL
6 tbsp	toasted shredded coconut	90 mL
2 tbsp	minced crystallized ginger	25 mL

1. In a saucepan over medium-low heat, melt butter. Add brown sugar, pineapple juice and rum; cook, stirring constantly, until sugar is dissolved. Increase heat to medium; bring to a boil and cook, stirring occasionally, for 5 minutes.

2. Remove saucepan from heat. Stir in nutmeg. Transfer immediately to dessert fondue pot over candle flame. Add toasted coconut and crystallized ginger. Stir well.

3. Spear a piece of fruit or cake with fondue fork and dip in fondue.

Serves 4 to 6

Tips

If the fondue appears too thick, add pineapple juice 1 tbsp (25 mL) at a time.

Single-serving juice boxes are ideal to have on hand for cooking purposes.

Make ahead

Prepare to end of Step 2. Cool, then refrigerate. Reheat in microwave on low until heated (about 1 to 2 minutes) or over low heat in saucepan on stove. Stir and transfer to fondue pot.

Cut up fruit and other dippers (except for bananas.)

Serve with...

Pineapple chunks, mango pieces, banana slices, angel food cake cubes, chocolate caramels.

Key Lime Fondue

Serves 4 to 6

Recipe tester Cheryl Warkentin perfected this recipe, which is reminiscent of key lime pie and is, as she puts it, "addictive."

Tip
If using a fondue pot other than one lit by a votive candle, ensure the flame is as low as possible.

Make ahead
Complete to the end of Step 2. Let cool, then refrigerate. Reheat in microwave on Low (1 to 2 minutes) or over low heat in a saucepan on the stovetop. Stir and transfer to fondue pot.

Cut up fruit and other dippers (except for bananas).

Serve with...
Banana slices, kiwi slices, strawberries, raspberries, ladyfingers, shortbread cookies, pound cake cubes, graham wafers, marshmallows.

10 oz	sweetened condensed milk	300 mL
	Grated zest of 12 key limes	
1/2 cup	freshly squeezed key lime juice (about 16 key limes)	125 mL
1/3 cup	water	75 mL
Pinch	salt	Pinch
1/2 tsp	vanilla	2 mL
2	egg yolks	2

1. In a medium saucepan, combine condensed milk and key lime juice; gradually stir in water, key lime zest and salt. Heat over low heat, whisking constantly until hot (do not boil). Stir in vanilla.

2. In a bowl, beat egg yolks. Stir in 1/3 cup (75 mL) of the key lime mixture; mix well. Return mixture to saucepan and whisk constantly over low heat until combined.

3. Remove from heat and transfer immediately to dessert fondue pot over candle flame.

4. Spear a piece of fruit or cake with fondue fork and dip in fondue.

Luscious Lemon Fondue

¾ cup	2% evaporated milk	175 mL
¾ cup	water	175 mL
½ cup	granulated sugar	125 mL
2½ tbsp	cornstarch	32 mL
	Grated zest and juice of 1 lemon	
Pinch	salt	Pinch
2	egg yolks	2

1. In a saucepan over medium heat, combine evaporated milk and water. Heat until hot, but do not boil. Reduce heat to low. Stir in sugar and cornstarch; cook, whisking constantly, until dissolved and mixture is thickened. Add lemon zest, lemon juice and salt; stir until thoroughly mixed.

2. In a bowl, beat egg yolks. Stir in about ⅓ cup (75 mL) of the lemon mixture. Return mixture to saucepan; cook, whisking constantly, until well mixed.

3. Transfer immediately to dessert fondue pot over candle flame.

4. Spear a piece of fruit or cake with fondue fork and dip in fondue.

Orange-Peach Fondue

Tip
For extra peach flavor, use peach schnapps in place of Grand Marnier.

Make ahead

Prepare to end of Step 1. Cool, then refrigerate. Reheat in microwave on low until heated (about 1 to 2 minutes) or over low heat in saucepan on stove. Stir and transfer to fondue pot.

Cut up fruit and other dippers (except for bananas.)

Serve with...
Dates, banana slices, pineapple chunks, angel food cake cubes, ladyfingers, banana bread chunks, or over ice cream.

½ cup	peach syrup from canned peaches (below)	125 mL
½ tsp	finely grated orange zest	2 mL
6 tbsp	freshly squeezed orange juice	90 mL
¼ cup	packed brown sugar	50 mL
¼ cup	water	50 mL
1 tbsp	cornstarch	15 mL
2	canned whole peaches, puréed	2
1 tbsp	Grand Marnier	15 mL
2	whole cloves (optional)	2
1	cinnamon stick	1

1. In a saucepan over medium heat, combine peach syrup, orange zest, orange juice, brown sugar, water and cornstarch. Bring to a boil, stirring constantly. Reduce heat to low. Add cloves and cinnamon stick. Simmer for 5 minutes.

2. Remove from heat. Discard cloves and cinnamon stick. Stir in puréed peaches and Grand Marnier. Transfer immediately to dessert fondue pot over candle flame.

3. Spear a piece of fruit or cake with fondue fork and dip in fondue.

Quick Jam Fondue

1 cup	seedless raspberry jam	250 mL
¼ cup	water	50 mL
2 tbsp	all-purpose flour	25 mL
2 tbsp	kirsch	25 mL
¼ tsp	finely grated lime zest	1 mL
1 tbsp	freshly squeezed lime juice	15 mL

1. In a saucepan over medium-low heat, stir together jam and water. Bring to a boil. Reduce heat to low and simmer for about 5 minutes, watching carefully to prevent scorching. Whisk in flour a little at a time and cook, whisking constantly, for another 5 minutes or until desired thickness is reached.

2. Remove from heat. Stir in kirsch, lime zest and lime juice. Transfer immediately to dessert fondue pot over candle flame.

3. Spear a piece of fruit or cake with fondue fork and dip in fondue.

Since this is a sweet fondue, you may want to serve it with plain bread cubes (à la cheese fondue) or other plain dippers.

Tip
You can substitute other varieties of jam or jelly for a different flavor — just make sure the product is seedless.

Make ahead
Prepare to end of Step 1. Cool, then refrigerate. Reheat in microwave on Low until heated (about 1 to 2 minutes) or over low heat in saucepan on stove. Stir and transfer to fondue pot.

Cut up fruit and other dippers (except for bananas).

Serve with...
Angel food cake cubes, ladyfingers, shortbread, vanilla biscuits, scone cubes, nuts.

Raspberry Fondue

Serves 4 to 6

14 oz	frozen raspberries in light syrup, thawed	425 g
2 tbsp	cornstarch	25 mL
2 tbsp	cold water	25 mL

Tips

Substitute frozen strawberries (or mixed berries) in syrup for the raspberries.

For a more intense flavor, stir 1/2 cup (125 mL) fresh berries into fondue pot just before serving.

For a lighter consistency, purée half of the raspberries before adding to saucepan.

Make ahead

Prepare to end of Step 2. Cool, then refrigerate. Reheat in microwave on Low until heated (about 1 to 2 minutes) or over low heat in saucepan on stove. Stir and transfer to fondue pot.

Cut up dippers.

Serve with...

Chocolate cupcake cubes, ladyfingers, shortbread cookies, scone cubes.

1. In a sieve over a bowl, drain raspberries, reserving 1 cup (250 mL) syrup. In another bowl, whisk together cornstarch and water until dissolved.

2. In a saucepan over medium heat, warm reserved syrup for about 3 minutes. Add dissolved cornstarch and continue heating for 2 minutes or until thickened.

3. Remove from heat. Stir in raspberries; mix well. Transfer immediately to dessert fondue pot over candle flame.

4. Spear a piece of fruit or cake with fondue fork and dip in fondue.

Caramel Fondue (page 225)

Luscious Lemon Fondue (page 237)

Orange-Peach Fondue (page 238)

Raspberry Fondue (page 240)

Dips and Sauces

Blue Cheese Dip

Tip

To reduce fat, replace mayonnaise with plain yogurt or light mayonnaise and use light instead of regular sour cream.

¼ cup	sour cream	50 mL
3 tbsp	mayonnaise	45 mL
4 oz	Roquefort cheese, crumbled	125 g
½ tsp	dried tarragon	2 mL
¼ tsp	hot pepper sauce (optional)	1 mL

1. In a bowl, combine sour cream, mayonnaise and Roquefort; mix well. Stir in tarragon and hot pepper sauce (if using). Cover and refrigerate until needed.

Honey Dill Dip

Makes 1 cup (250 mL)

²⁄₃ cup	mayonnaise	150 mL
¹⁄₃ cup	liquid honey	75 mL
½ tsp	dried dillweed	2 mL

1. In a bowl, combine mayonnaise, honey and dill; mix well. Cover and refrigerate until needed.

Horseradish Dip

¼ cup	prepared horseradish	50 mL	
¼ cup	mayonnaise	50 mL	**Makes 1 cup (250 mL)**
¼ cup	sour cream	50 mL	
1 tbsp	freshly squeezed lemon juice	15 mL	
¾ tsp	granulated sugar	4 mL	

1. In a bowl, combine horseradish, mayonnaise, sour cream, lemon juice and sugar; mix well. Cover and refrigerate overnight to allow flavors to blend. Bring to room temperature before serving.

Lemon Dill Dip

¾ cup	plain yogurt	175 mL	
3 tbsp	minced fresh dill	45 mL	**Makes ¾ cup (175 mL)**
1 tbsp	grated lemon zest	15 mL	
½ tsp	lemon pepper	2 mL	
¼ tsp	salt	1 mL	

1. In a bowl, combine yogurt, dill, lemon zest, lemon pepper and salt; mix well. Cover and refrigerate for at least 1 hour before serving, or until needed.

Mint Yogurt Dip

Makes ¾ cup (175 mL)			
¾ cup	plain 1% yogurt		175 mL
2 tbsp	minced English cucumber		25 mL
1	clove garlic, minced		1
4 tsp	chopped fresh mint		20 mL
	Salt and freshly ground black pepper to taste		

1. In a fine-mesh sieve or cheesecloth set over a bowl, drain yogurt for 15 minutes. Discard liquid in bowl.

2. Place minced cucumber in strainer and strain for 10 minutes to remove excess liquid.

3. In another bowl, combine thickened yogurt, cucumber, garlic and mint. Season with salt and pepper; mix well. Cover and refrigerate for at least 30 minutes before serving.

Roasted Red Pepper Dip

Makes ¾ cup (175 mL)		
2	red bell peppers, roasted, peeled, seeded and chopped	2
1	clove garlic, minced	1
½ cup	plain yogurt	125 mL
½ cup	sour cream	125 mL
¼ cup	chopped fresh parsley	50 mL
2 tbsp	chopped fresh basil	25 mL
1 tbsp	chopped fresh oregano	15 mL
1½ tbsp	freshly squeezed lemon juice	22 mL
¾ tsp	hot pepper sauce	4 mL

1. In a bowl, combine peppers, garlic, yogurt, sour cream, parsley, basil, oregano, lemon juice and hot pepper sauce; mix well. Cover and refrigerate until needed. Bring to room temperature before serving.

Sweet Mustard Dip

4 tbsp	dry mustard	60 mL
4 tbsp	cold water	60 mL
3 to 4 tbsp	packed brown sugar	45 to 60 mL

Makes ¼ cup (50 mL)

1. In a bowl, whisk together mustard and water until mixture has the consistency of thick cream. Stir in 3 tbsp (45 mL) brown sugar or more, to taste. Cover and refrigerate until needed. Bring to room temperature before serving.

Sweet Thai Dip

6 tbsp	water	90 mL
¼ cup	granulated sugar	50 mL
¼ cup	chopped fresh cilantro	50 mL
2 tbsp	chili garlic sauce	25 mL
2 tbsp	freshly squeezed lime juice	25 mL
2 tsp	fish sauce (see tip, page 189)	10 mL

Makes ½ cup (125 mL)

1. In a bowl, whisk together water and sugar until dissolved. Add cilantro, chili garlic sauce, lime juice and fish sauce; mix well. Allow flavors to blend for at least 30 minutes. Cover and refrigerate until needed. Bring to room temperature before serving.

Hummus

<table>
<tr><td>Makes 1 cup
(250 mL)</td><td>2</td><td>cloves garlic</td><td>2</td></tr>
<tr><td></td><td>1</td><td>can (19 oz/540 mL) chickpeas, drained and rinsed</td><td>1</td></tr>
<tr><td></td><td>3 tbsp</td><td>tahini</td><td>45 mL</td></tr>
<tr><td></td><td></td><td>Juice of 1 lemon</td><td></td></tr>
<tr><td></td><td>3 tbsp</td><td>olive oil</td><td>45 mL</td></tr>
<tr><td></td><td>½ tsp</td><td>cumin seeds</td><td>2 mL</td></tr>
<tr><td></td><td></td><td>Salt and freshly black ground pepper to taste</td><td></td></tr>
</table>

1. In a food processor, mince garlic. Add chickpeas, tahini and lemon juice; process until combined. With the motor running, through the feed tube, slowly drizzle in olive oil. Add cumin seeds, salt and pepper; pulse until smooth. Cover and refrigerate overnight to let flavors blend. Bring to room temperature before serving.

Tzatziki

<table>
<tr><td>Makes 1½ cups
(375 mL)</td><td>1 cup</td><td>plain yogurt</td><td>250 mL</td></tr>
<tr><td></td><td>2</td><td>cloves garlic, minced</td><td>2</td></tr>
<tr><td></td><td>½</td><td>English cucumber, peeled and diced</td><td>½</td></tr>
<tr><td></td><td>2 tbsp</td><td>freshly squeezed lemon juice</td><td>25 mL</td></tr>
<tr><td></td><td>1 tbsp</td><td>chopped fresh dill</td><td>15 mL</td></tr>
<tr><td></td><td></td><td>Salt and freshly ground black pepper to taste</td><td></td></tr>
</table>

1. In a fine-mesh sieve or cheesecloth set over a bowl, drain yogurt overnight. Discard liquid in bowl.

2. In a bowl, combine thickened yogurt, garlic, cucumber, lemon juice, dill, salt and pepper; mix well. Cover and refrigerate for at least 1 hour or for up to 1 day before serving.

Salsa Verde

2	cloves garlic	2
¾ cup	chopped fresh cilantro	175 mL
½ cup	chopped fresh parsley	125 mL
3 tbsp	olive oil	45 mL
1 tsp	finely grated lime zest	5 mL
1 tbsp	freshly squeezed lime juice	15 mL
1 tbsp	finely minced jalapeño	15 mL
1 tbsp	minced green onion (white part only)	15 mL
Pinch	salt	Pinch

Makes 1 cup (250 mL)

1. In a food processor, combine garlic, cilantro, parsley, oil, lime zest, lime juice, jalapeño, green onion and salt; process until well blended. Cover and refrigerate for at least 2 hours before serving, or until needed.

Mango Salsa

1	large mango, peeled and chopped	1
1	clove garlic, minced	1
1	jalapeño pepper, minced	1
½ cup	chopped fresh cilantro	125 mL
¼ cup	minced onion	50 mL
2 tbsp	freshly squeezed lime juice	25 mL
2 tbsp	olive oil	25 mL
	Salt and freshly ground black pepper to taste	

Makes 1½ cups (375 mL)

1. In a bowl, combine mango, garlic, jalapeño, cilantro, onion, lime juice, oil, salt and pepper; mix well. Cover and refrigerate overnight to allow flavors to blend. Bring to room temperature before serving.

Cilantro Coulis

Makes ½ cup (125 mL)

1	clove garlic	1
¾ cup	chopped fresh cilantro	175 mL
2 tbsp	purple onion	25 mL
1 tbsp	granulated sugar	15 mL
2 tsp	diced seeded jalapeño pepper	10 mL
¾ tsp	ground cumin	4 mL
	Juice of 1 lime	

1. In a food processor, mince garlic. Add cilantro, onion, sugar, jalapeño, cumin and lime juice; process just until mixed (coulis should be coarse). Cover and refrigerate until needed.

Gremolata

Makes ½ cup (125 mL)

2	cloves garlic, minced	2
½ cup	chopped fresh parsley	125 mL
1 tbsp	minced lemon zest	15 mL

1. In a bowl, combine garlic, parsley and lemon zest; mix well. Cover and refrigerate until needed.

Spicy Sesame Mayonnaise

¼ cup	mayonnaise	50 mL
1 tbsp	vinegar	15 mL
1 tsp	granulated sugar	5 mL
1	clove garlic, minced	1
2 tbsp	minced candied ginger	25 mL
1 tbsp	sesame seeds, toasted	15 mL

Makes ⅓ cup (75 mL)

1. In a bowl, whisk together mayonnaise, vinegar and sugar; mix well. Stir in garlic, candied ginger and sesame seeds; mix well. Cover and refrigerate for at least 30 minutes before serving, or until needed.

Wasabi Mayonnaise

½ cup	mayonnaise	125 mL
1 tbsp	wasabi powder	15 mL

Makes ½ cup (125 mL)

1. In a bowl, combine mayonnaise and wasabi; mix well. Cover and refrigerate for at least 1 hour to allow flavors to blend, or until needed. Bring to room temperature before serving.

Zesty Mayonnaise

Makes 1 cup (250 mL)	1 cup	mayonnaise	250 mL
	1 tsp	paprika	5 mL
	¼ tsp	cayenne pepper	1 mL

1. In a bowl, combine mayonnaise, paprika and cayenne pepper; mix well. Cover and refrigerate until needed.

Dijonnaise (Mustard Mayonnaise)

Makes ¾ cup (175 mL)	⅔ cup	sour cream	150 mL
	2 tbsp	mayonnaise	25 mL
	1 tbsp	Dijon mustard	15 mL

1. In a bowl, combine sour cream, mayonnaise and Dijon mustard; mix well. Cover and refrigerate for at least 1 hour before serving, or until needed.

Honey Mustard

¼ cup	liquid honey	50 mL
¼ cup	Dijon mustard	50 mL
	Salt and freshly ground black pepper to taste	

Makes ½ cup (125 mL)

1. In a bowl, whisk together honey and mustard. Season with salt and pepper. Cover and refrigerate until needed. Bring to room temperature or heat briefly in the microwave on Low before serving.

Quick Garlic Aïoli

2	cloves garlic, minced	2
1 cup	prepared mayonnaise	250 mL
Pinch	kosher salt	Pinch

Makes 1 cup (250 mL)

1. In a bowl, combine garlic, mayonnaise and salt; mix well. Cover and refrigerate until needed.

Red Pepper Aïoli

**Makes ½ cup
(125 mL)**

1	clove garlic	1
1	roasted red pepper (see tips, page 58), peeled, seeded and quartered	1
2 tbsp	chopped fresh parsley	25 mL
1 tbsp	olive oil	1
1 tsp	freshly squeezed lemon juice	5 mL
4	drops chipotle-flavored hot pepper sauce	4
	Salt and freshly ground black pepper to taste	

1. In a food processor, mince garlic. Add roasted pepper, parsley, olive oil, lemon juice, hot pepper sauce, salt and black pepper; process until smooth. Cover and refrigerate until needed. Bring to room temperature before serving.

Lemon Sauce

**Makes 1 cup
(250 mL)**

⅓ cup	chicken broth (store-bought or see recipe, page 127)	75 mL
1½ tbsp	cornstarch	22 mL
½ cup	freshly squeezed lemon juice	125 mL
2 tbsp	light soy sauce	25 mL
1 tsp	sesame oil	5 mL

1. In a small bowl, whisk together chicken broth and cornstarch until dissolved.

2. In a saucepan over medium-low heat, combine lemon juice, soy sauce and cornstarch mixture; cook, stirring constantly, until sauce thickens. Stir in sesame oil. Remove from heat and let cool.

3. Cover and refrigerate until needed. To serve, warm in microwave for 1 minute on Low.

Shrimp Cocktail Sauce

1	clove garlic	1	**Makes ½ cup (125 mL)**
⅓ cup	chili sauce	75 mL	
3 tbsp	white vinegar	45 mL	
1½ tbsp	prepared horseradish	22 mL	
1 tbsp	granulated sugar	15 mL	

1. In a food processor, mince garlic. Add chili sauce, vinegar, horseradish and sugar; pulse until well combined and smooth. Cover and refrigerate until needed.

Sweet-and-Sour Sauce

2 tbsp	water (approx.)	25 mL	**Makes 1 cup (250 mL)**
1 tbsp	cornstarch	15 mL	
½ cup	ketchup	125 mL	
½ cup	vinegar	125 mL	
⅓ cup	packed brown sugar	75 mL	

1. In a small bowl, whisk together water and cornstarch until dissolved.

2. In a saucepan over medium heat, combine ketchup, vinegar and brown sugar. Bring to a boil. Add dissolved cornstarch; stir until thickened, adding more water as required to reach desired consistency. Remove from heat and let cool.

3. Cover and refrigerate until needed. Heat in microwave on Low before serving.

Tonkatsu Sauce

Makes ½ cup (125 mL)		
¼ cup	ketchup	50 mL
1½ tbsp	soy sauce	22 mL
1½ tbsp	seasoned rice vinegar	22 mL
1 tbsp	Worcestershire sauce	15 mL
1 tbsp	granulated sugar	15 mL
¼ tsp	ground ginger	1 mL
¼ tsp	garlic powder	1 mL

1. In a bowl, whisk together ketchup, soy sauce, vinegar, Worcestershire sauce, sugar, ginger and garlic powder; mix well. Cover and refrigerate until needed.

Asian Dipping Sauce

Makes ⅔ cup (150 mL)		
¼ cup	Japanese soy sauce	50 mL
¼ cup	regular soy sauce	50 mL
2 tbsp	sake	25 mL
1½ tbsp	granulated sugar	22 mL
1 tbsp	fish sauce	15 mL
1 tbsp	freshly squeezed lime juice	15 mL
1 tbsp	rice vinegar	15 mL
1 tbsp	sesame oil	15 mL

Tip

For a spicier version, add 2 tsp (10 mL) chili garlic sauce.

1. In a bowl, whisk together Japanese soy sauce, regular soy sauce, sake, sugar, fish sauce, lime juice, vinegar and sesame oil. Cover and refrigerate until needed.

Mongolian Hot Pot Dipping Sauce

2	cloves garlic, minced	2
¾ cup	soy sauce	175 mL
3 tbsp	rice vinegar	45 mL
2 tbsp	sesame oil	25 mL
1 tbsp	dry sherry	15 mL
2 tsp	sake	10 mL
2 tsp	chili garlic sauce	10 mL

Makes 1 cup (250 mL)

1. In a bowl, whisk together garlic, soy sauce, vinegar, sesame oil, sherry, sake and chili garlic sauce. Cover and refrigerate until needed.

Thai Peanut Sauce

2	cloves garlic, minced	2
¼ cup	liquid honey	50 mL
2 tbsp	rice vinegar	25 mL
2 tbsp	smooth peanut butter	25 mL
2 tbsp	soy sauce	25 mL
2 tbsp	vegetable oil	25 mL
1 tbsp	sesame oil	15 mL
2 tsp	minced gingerroot	10 mL
½ tsp	hot pepper flakes	2 mL

Makes ¾ cup (175 mL)

1. In a bowl, combine garlic, honey, vinegar, peanut butter, soy sauce, vegetable oil, sesame oil, ginger and hot pepper flakes; mix well. Cover and refrigerate until needed.

Tomato Curry Sauce

Makes 1½ cups (375 mL)		
1	can (14 oz/398 mL) diced tomatoes, with juice	1
¼ cup	water	50 mL
1 tbsp	tomato paste	15 mL
2 tsp	all-purpose flour	10 mL
1 tsp	packed brown sugar	5 mL
1 tsp	ground cumin	5 mL
¾ tsp	ground turmeric	4 mL
½ tsp	dry mustard	2 mL
½ tsp	ground ginger	2 mL
¼ tsp	cayenne pepper	1 mL

1. In a saucepan over medium heat, combine tomatoes, with juice, water, tomato paste, flour, brown sugar, cumin, turmeric, mustard, ginger and cayenne pepper. Bring to a boil. Reduce heat to low and cook, stirring occasionally, for 30 minutes. Remove from heat and let cool.

2. Cover and refrigerate until needed. Warm up in microwave or over low heat on stove before serving.

Library and Archives Canada Cataloguing in Publication

Simon, Ilana, 1963–
    The fondue bible : the 200 best recipes / Ilana Simon.

Includes index.
ISBN 978-0-7788-0166-5

    1. Fondue. I. Title.

TX825.S53 2007   641.8'1   C2007-903024-6

Index

More Great Books
from Robert Rose

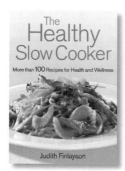

Appliance Cooking

- 125 Best Microwave Oven Recipes
  by Johanna Burkhard
- The Blender Bible
  by Andrew Chase and Nicole Young
- The Mixer Bible
  by Meredith Deeds and Carla Snyder
- The 150 Best Slow Cooker Recipes
  by Judith Finlayson
- Delicious & Dependable Slow Cooker Recipes
  by Judith Finlayson
- 125 Best Vegetarian Slow Cooker Recipes
  by Judith Finlayson
- The Healthy Slow Cooker
  by Judith Finlayson
- 125 Best Rotisserie Oven Recipes
  by Judith Finlayson
- 125 Best Food Processor Recipes
  by George Geary
- The Best Family Slow Cooker Recipes
  by Donna-Marie Pye
- The Best Convection Oven Cookbook
  by Linda Stephen
- 250 Best American Bread Machine Baking Recipes
  by Donna Washburn and Heather Butt
- 250 Best Canadian Bread Machine Baking Recipes
  by Donna Washburn and Heather Butt

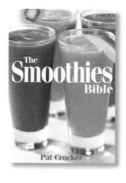

Baking

- 250 Best Cakes & Pies
  by Esther Brody
- 500 Best Cookies, Bars & Squares
  by Esther Brody
- 500 Best Muffin Recipes
  by Esther Brody
- 125 Best Cheesecake Recipes
  by George Geary
- 125 Best Chocolate Recipes
  by Julie Hasson
- 125 Best Chocolate Chip Recipes
  by Julie Hasson
- 125 Best Cupcake Recipes
  by Julie Hasson
- Complete Cake Mix Magic
  by Jill Snider

Healthy Cooking

- 125 Best Vegetarian Recipes
  by Byron Ayanoglu with contributions from Algis Kemezys
- America's Best Cookbook for Kids with Diabetes
  by Colleen Bartley
- Canada's Best Cookbook for Kids with Diabetes
  by Colleen Bartley
- The Juicing Bible
  by Pat Crocker and Susan Eagles
- The Smoothies Bible
  by Pat Crocker

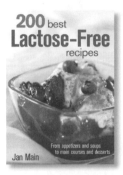

- 125 Best Vegan Recipes
  by Maxine Effenson Chuck and Beth Gurney
- 200 Best Lactose-Free Recipes
  by Jan Main
- 500 Best Healthy Recipes
  Edited by Lynn Roblin, RD
- 125 Best Gluten-Free Recipes
  by Donna Washburn and Heather Butt
- The Best Gluten-Free Family Cookbook
  by Donna Washburn and Heather Butt
- America's Everyday Diabetes Cookbook
  Edited by Katherine E. Younker, MBA, RD
- Canada's Everyday Diabetes Choice Recipes
  Edited by Katherine E. Younker, MBA, RD
- America's Complete Diabetes Cookbook
  Edited by Katherine E. Younker, MBA, RD
- Canada's Complete Diabetes Cookbook
  Edited by Katherine E. Younker, MBA, RD

Recent Bestsellers

- 125 Best Soup Recipes
  by Marylin Crowley and Joan Mackie
- The Convenience Cook
  by Judith Finlayson
- 125 Best Ice Cream Recipes
  by Marilyn Linton and Tanya Linton

- Easy Indian Cooking
  by Suneeta Vaswani
- Baby Blender Food
  by Nicole Young
- Simply Thai Cooking
  by Wandee Young and Byron Ayanoglu

Health

- The Complete Natural Medicine Guide to the 50 Most Common Medicinal Herbs
  by Dr. Heather Boon, B.Sc.Phm., Ph.D., and Michael Smith, B.Pharm, M.R.Pharm.S., ND
- The Complete Natural Medicine Guide to Breast Cancer
  by Sat Dharam Kaur, ND
- Better Food for Pregnancy
  by Daina Kalnins, MSc, RD, and Joanne Saab, RD
- Help for Eating Disorders
  by Dr. Debra Katzman, MD, FRCP(C), and Dr. Leora Pinhas, MD
- The Complete Doc[...] Healthy Back Bible[...]
  by Dr. Stephen Reed, and Penny Kendall-[...] MSc, ND, with Dr. [...] Ford, MD, FRCSC, Dr. Charles Gregor[...] MD, ChB, FRCP([...]
- Crohn's & Col[...]
  by Dr. A. Hillary [...] MD, MSc, FRC[...]
- Chronic Hea[...]
  by Barbara E. [...] MSc, RD, and [...] Ruffolo

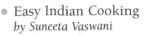

Wherever books are sold

Fo[...]

- 125 Best Vegan Recipes
  by Maxine Effenson Chuck and Beth Gurney
- 200 Best Lactose-Free Recipes
  by Jan Main
- 500 Best Healthy Recipes
  Edited by Lynn Roblin, RD
- 125 Best Gluten-Free Recipes
  by Donna Washburn and Heather Butt
- The Best Gluten-Free Family Cookbook
  by Donna Washburn and Heather Butt
- America's Everyday Diabetes Cookbook
  Edited by Katherine E. Younker, MBA, RD
- Canada's Everyday Diabetes Choice Recipes
  Edited by Katherine E. Younker, MBA, RD
- America's Complete Diabetes Cookbook
  Edited by Katherine E. Younker, MBA, RD
- Canada's Complete Diabetes Cookbook
  Edited by Katherine E. Younker, MBA, RD

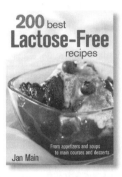

Recent Bestsellers

- 125 Best Soup Recipes
  by Marylin Crowley and Joan Mackie
- The Convenience Cook
  by Judith Finlayson
- 125 Best Ice Cream Recipes
  by Marilyn Linton and Tanya Linton

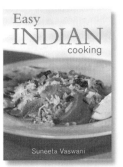

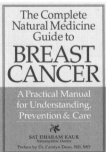

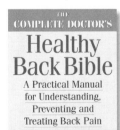

- Easy Indian Cooking
  by Suneeta Vaswani
- Baby Blender Food
  by Nicole Young
- Simply Thai Cooking
  by Wandee Young and Byron Ayanoglu

Health

- The Complete Natural Medicine Guide to the 50 Most Common Medicinal Herbs
  by Dr. Heather Boon, B.Sc.Phm., Ph.D., and Michael Smith, B.Pharm, M.R.Pharm.S., ND
- The Complete Natural Medicine Guide to Breast Cancer
  by Sat Dharam Kaur, ND
- Better Food for Pregnancy
  by Daina Kalnins, MSc, RD, and Joanne Saab, RD
- Help for Eating Disorders
  by Dr. Debra Katzman, MD, FRCP(C), and Dr. Leora Pinhas, MD
- The Complete Doctor's Healthy Back Bible
  by Dr. Stephen Reed, MD, and Penny Kendall-Reed, MSc, ND, with Dr. Michael Ford, MD, FRCSC, and Dr. Charles Gregory, MD, ChB, FRCP(C)
- Crohn's & Colitis
  by Dr. A. Hillary Steinhart, MD, MSc, FRCP(C)
- Chronic Heartburn
  by Barbara E. Wendland, MSc, RD, and Lisa Marie Ruffolo